H. L. Mencken

H. L. Mencken

Vincent Fitzpatrick

Mercer University Press
Macon, Georgia

ISBN 0-86554-921-4
MUP/H639

Originally published by The Continuum Publishing Company, 1989.

∞The paper used in this publication meets the minimum requirements of
American National Standard for Information Sciences—Permanence of Paper
for Printed Library Materials, ANSI Z39.48-1992.

Library of Congress Cataloging-in-Publication Data

Fitzpatrick, Vincent.
 H.L. Mencken / Vincent Fitzpatrick.
    p. cm.
Includes bibliographical references and index.
 ISBN 0-86554-921-4 (hardcover : alk. paper)
1. Mencken, H. L. (Henry Louis), 1880-1956--Criticism and interpretation.
2. Mencken, H. L. (Henry Louis), 1880-1956--Knowledge--Literature.
3. American literature--History and criticism—Theory, etc. 4. Criticism—
United States—History—20th century. I. Title.
 PS3525.E43Z554 2004
 818'.5209—dc22
                                                                    2003027112

In memory of John Thompson (1918-2002)

Contents

Preface

"I have written and printed probably 10,000,000 words of English," Henry Louis Mencken declared in 1940, "and continue to this day to pour out more and more. It has wrung from others, some of them my superiors, probably a million words of notice, part of it pro but most of it con. In brief, my booth has been set up on a favorable pitch, and I have never lacked hearers for my ballyhoo."[1] This pitchman, to borrow Mencken's waggish metaphor, performed for half a century, from 1899 to 1948. In addition to his thousands of newspaper columns, book reviews, and essays, he contributed to more than twenty books and wrote in excess of forty. Several appreciably influenced American letters and life.

Once he discovered his authentic voice, Mencken was able to popularize his material without vulgarizing it. He thereby succeeded at one of the writer's most difficult tasks: he was simultaneously intelligible to the general reader and informative to the professional. Ours is an age of literary specialization, perhaps of literary safety. To us, the range of Mencken's interests, the diversity of his audience, and the number of roles he played seem staggering.[2]

Mencken wrote about nearly everything: from literature to economics, from politics to food, from religion to World War I,

---

[1]Mencken, *Happy Days: 1880–1892* (New York: Knopf, 1940) 198.

[2]Mencken's diversity has been acknowledged by nearly all the critics who have discussed his canon. See especially W. H. A. Williams's preface to *H. L. Mencken* (Boston: Twayne, 1977). In terms of readership, there is a similarity between Mencken's career and that of Edmund Wilson, Mencken's junior by fifteen years.

from the music of Beethoven to the heavyweight championship fight between boxers Jack Dempsey and Georges Carpentier. As a newspaperman—Mencken always considered himself foremost a journalist—he is associated most frequently with the Baltimore *Sunpapers*, but his writing also appeared in such newspapers as the New York *Evening Mail*, the *Chicago Tribune*, and the New York *American*. Mencken the autobiographer filled the *Days* trilogy with fond remembrances of a more colorful, less hurried past. *The American Language*, a tribute to Mencken's lifelong interest in philology, ran to four editions and two supplements. As an editor of magazines, Mencken saw the *American Mercury*, which he helped to establish in 1924, become highly successful and even more notorious. Mencken the literary critic has been likened to a pioneer, a pathfinder who helped to lead America out of her tangled, repressive past so that her writers could discuss the subjects of their choice in the language that best suited their ends. With his acute sense of the absurd, Mencken mastered the art of making people laugh. As an American humorist, he has been ranked second only to Mark Twain.[3] No matter what the subject, the majority of Mencken's writing was done in that highly individualistic style–alternately congenial and caustic, rollicking and admonitory–that has frequently been imitated and rarely equaled.

Three roles shaped such a diverse and productive career. Mencken remained above all else a civil libertarian, an "individualist" (to use his own term), and an iconoclast. He insisted upon the individual's right to be left alone and saw freedom of speech, up to "the limits of the unendurable," as the most valuable attribute of any society.[4] While other Americans

---

[3]R. P. Harriss, "Dear Mencken, Thanks for the Memories," Baltimore *News American*, 11 September 1977.

[4]Mencken labels himself an "individualist" in the subtitle of *Men Versus the Man*, his epistolary debate with the Socialist Robert Rives La Monte (New

sought the safety of the fold, Mencken challenged a number of powerful opponents. Some of Mencken's contemporaries, for example, deified Woodrow Wilson, William Jennings Bryan, and Franklin Delano Roosevelt, but Mencken viewed these men—two presidents and a man nominated three times for that office—as liar, fool, and thief, respectively. "The liberation of the human mind," roared the brazen Mencken, "has been furthered by gay fellows who heaved dead cats into sanctuaries and then went roistering down the highways of the world, proving to all men that doubt, after all, was safe—that the god in his sanctuary was finite in his power and hence a fraud."[5] To those who wondered why Mencken, finding so little worthy of respect, continued to live in America, he answered with characteristic glee: "Why do men go to zoos?"[6]

This heaver of dead cats has proven one of the more controversial figures in the history of American letters. To some critics, Mencken was a demi-god, a figure compared favorably to Voltaire, Samuel Johnson, and George Bernard Shaw. Mencken's prose has been called "the best...ever written in America during the twentieth century."[7] On the other hand, Mencken's many detractors vilified him; few Americans have been bludgeoned so violently in print. He was lambasted as a poorly educated ruffian, alternately crude and cruel. One of Mencken's articles so incensed the citizens of Arkansas that the state legislature wanted him deported. One critic called Mencken

---

York: Holt, 1910). He made the quoted remark about freedom of speech during a recorded interview in 1948, released as *H. L. Mencken Speaks* by Caedmon Records (TC-1082).

[5]Mencken, "The Iconoclast," in *Prejudices: Fourth Series* (New York: Knopf, 1924) 139–40.

[6]Mencken, "Catechism," in *A Mencken Chrestomathy* (New York: Knopf, 1949) 627.

[7]Joseph Wood Krutch, "This Was Mencken: An Appreciation," *The Nation* 182 (11 February 1956): 109–10.

"the boy-pervert from Baltimore," and another likened him, rabid at his typewriter, to a dog tearing at a snake.[8]

This productive and controversial career also generated a number of contradictions. Some grew from the curious ways in which Mencken's writing was interpreted. This Jeffersonian liberal, for example, was pilloried as both a radical and a reactionary. The pronounced difference between Mencken's life and work spawned other contradictions. The political critic who railed at what he viewed as the futility and pernicious effects of public charity was a very generous private citizen. This brazen, booming writer, who terrified some opponents and infuriated others, behaved as a "basically romantic, sentimental, and emotionally Victorian man."[9] Dissenting from ideas rather than from decorum, Mencken paid his bills promptly, worked every day, kept in the good graces of the law, and bought candy for the neighborhood children. Mencken served, in short, as a highly respectable citizen of the nation whose name he so often took in vain. Indeed, the writer who expressed such profound skepticism about the American way of life methodically carved out a career that stands as a monument to the American dream.

The present study will, I hope, be accessible to the college student and general reader as well as informative to the scholar. Given its relative brevity, this book cannot offer a comprehensive account of such a productive, disputatious, and sometimes problematic career. Instead, I have tried to account for the marked influence that Mencken had upon American life and letters by discussing his most accomplished and influential writing, setting forth his major relationships, and briefly plotting the significant battles. Following the initial biographical chapter,

---

[8]Mencken, *Menckeniana: A Schimpflexikon* (New York: Knopf, 1928) 19, 7.

[9] Sara Mayfield, *The Constant Circle: H. L. Mencken and His Friends* (New York: Delacorte Press, 1968) 60.

I have used a chronological structure rather than a topical one. The rise, fall, and rebirth of Mencken's popularity are best understood, I think, in the context of changes in the twentieth-century American scene. Mencken's story, in the end, tells us a good deal about ourselves.

The interest that Mencken's writing generated during his career has continued since his death in 1956. A number of anthologies have appeared, as have numerous collections of his correspondence. He has been the subject of a variety of studies both general and particular in nature. Books have been devoted to such specifics as his editing of the *American Mercury*, his response to the American South, his role as a satirist, his literary criticism, his assistance to African-American authors, and his social criticism. Space precludes extensive analyses here of such matters, and I have used the footnotes to direct interested readers to a more comprehensive discussion of the issue at hand.

This volume was first published, under this title, by the Continuum Publishing Company of New York City in 1989. I am grateful for their kindness in allowing this book to be reissued by the Mercer University Press. I have made some relatively minor changes in the text by correcting typographical errors, solecisms, and some errors in fact. I have added a variety of photographs, expanded the chronology, updated the notes and bibliography, and written an "Afterword" that assesses Mencken's growing canon and the response to it during the past fifteen years. This has proven, to say the least, a very productive and lively time.

Portions of this book have appeared in different form in *H. L. M., The Mencken Bibliography: A Second Ten-Year Supplement, 1972–1981*; *Menckeniana*; and the *Virginia Quarterly Review*. I am grateful for permission to use this material. I am also grateful to the Enoch Pratt Free Library in Baltimore, the executor of Mencken's literary estate, for permission to use the photographs of Mencken and to quote from his writing. I wish to thank the estate of Theodore Dreiser for permission to quote from his writing.

I would like to acknowledge the generous assistance of several people. I particularly want to thank Mrs. Averil Kadis for her kind assistance. Charles A. Fecher, former editor of the quarterly *Menckeniana*, author of *Mencken: A Study of His Thought*, and editor of *The Diary of H. L. Mencken*, generously read my manuscript in its entirety. He saved me from error more than once and suggested judgments and interpretations that led me to reconsider several of my own. I am grateful to Carl Bode, the eminent Mencken scholar, for his assistance and support over a number of years. (Dr. Bode passed away in 1993; *Thirty-Five Years of Newspaper Work: A Memoir by H. L. Mencken* is dedicated to his memory.) Several conversations with Thomas B. Riggio, the editor of the Dreiser-Mencken correspondence, were most enlightening. So were numerous conversations with Fred Hobson, author of the distinguished biography *Mencken: A Life*. I would like to thank Richard J. Schrader for his generous and expert assistance with the bibliography. I am grateful to John Innes, an expert in the German language, for his kind assistance over a number of years. I am grateful to those who kindly contributed blurbs for the dust jacket: Fred Hobson, Carl Bode, Charles Fecher, and Terry Teachout.

My colleagues in the Enoch Pratt Free Library's Humanities Department assisted in ways too numerous to mention here. I extend my thanks to all. Kenneth White of the Enoch Pratt Free Library proved, as always, most helpful in securing material for me through interlibrary loan; I appreciate his expertise and generosity. I am grateful to Evander Lomke, my editor at Continuum, for his guidance and support. I appreciate the expert assistance offered by my editors at Mercer University Press,

Marc Jolley and Edmon L. Rowell, Jr. and by Publishing
Assistant Marsha M. Luttrell.

Finally, I want to thank my wife and fellow author, Carol,
and our son, Michael. Carol's editorial skills far surpass my own,
and more than once she has guided me out of mazes of my own
creation. She knows well the difference between good prose and
bad and, bless her, always tells me the truth. Carol and Mike
have been remarkably tolerant of the man who sits alone at the
computer and writes about the deceased, the man who has taken
them on vacations that have included visits to manuscript
collections and graveyards, the man who thinks too much about
Mencken's Baltimore and too little about his own.

When *H. L. Mencken* was first published in 1989, it was
dedicated to John Thompson. Unfortunately, the dedication of
the present volume is an *in memoriam*. Professor Thompson died
in New York City on June 24, 2002. He was my advisor in the
English Department of the State University of New York at
Stony Brook. A person of rare intelligence, he wrote like an
angel, and he generously took the time to teach a callow graduate
student what he needed to learn in order to write professionally. I
was blessed to have him as a mentor.

Chronology

1880 Henry Louis Mencken is born September 12 in Baltimore, the first of four children, to August and Anna Abhau Mencken.

1883 Mencken family moves to 1524 Hollins Street.

1896 Graduates at fifteen from the Baltimore Polytechnic Institute, a high school (end of formal education); enters family cigar business.

1899 After father's death on January 13, Mencken begins journalism career as reporter for the Baltimore *Morning Herald*.

1901 Becomes drama critic of the *Herald*, September, and editor of the *Sunday Herald,* October.

1903 Becomes city editor of the *Morning Herald*, October; *Ventures into Verse* published.

1904 Becomes city editor of *Evening Herald*, August; covers first presidential convention.

1905 Becomes managing editor of *Herald*; publication of *George Bernard Shaw: His Plays*.

1906 *Herald* folds June 17; serves as news editor, Baltimore *Evening News*, June–July; joins Baltimore *Sunday Sun*, July 25.

1908 First trip to Europe; begins to write book reviews for the *Smart Set*, November; publication of *The Philosophy of Friedrich Nietzsche*.

1909 Edits and writes introductions and notes to Henrik Ibsen's *A Doll's House* and *Little Eyolf.*

1910 Helps to establish the Baltimore *Evening Sun* (April 18) and is appointed associate editor; ghostwrites Leonard

Hirshberg's *What You Ought to Know About Your Baby*;
publication of *The Gist of Nietzsche*, arranged by Mencken;
publication of *Men Versus the Man*, an epistolary debate
with Robert Rives La Monte.

1911 Begins "The Free Lance" column in the Baltimore *Evening
Sun*, May 8 (continues until 23 October 1915).

1912 Trip to England, France, Switzerland, Germany, April;
publication of *The Artist: A Drama Without Words*.

1914 Publication of *Europe After 8:15*, with George Jean Nathan
and Willard Huntington Wright; Mencken and Nathan
become co-editors of the *Smart Set*, October.

1916 Defends Theodore Dreiser's *The "Genius"* against charges
of lewdness and profanity; publication of *A Book of
Burlesques* and *A Little Book in C Major*; sails to England,
December 28, proceeds to Germany to report on World War
I.

1917 Returns to America in March; begins to write for the New
York *Evening Mail*, June 18 (column continues until 8 July
1918); publication of *A Book of Prefaces* and *Pistols for
Two*, written with George Jean Nathan under the
pseudonym "Owen Hatteras."

1918 Publication of *Damn! A Book of Calumny* and *In Defense
of Women*.

1919 Publication of *The American Language* (First Edition) and
Prejudices: First Series.

1920 Begins "Monday Articles" in Baltimore *Evening Sun*
(column continues until 31 January 1938); covers
Republican National Convention, Chicago, June; covers
Democratic National Convention, San Francisco, June–July;
publication of *Prejudices: Second Series*, *The American
Credo* and *Heliogabalus* (latter two written with George
Jean Nathan); publication of *The Anti-Christ* by Friedrich
Nietzsche, translated and with an introduction by Mencken.

1921 Publication of *The American Language* (Second Edition).

1922 Publication of *Prejudices: Third Series*.

1923 Meets Sara Powell Haardt of Montgomery, Alabama, and Goucher College, his wife-to-be, May; Mencken and Nathan resign as co-editors of the *Smart Set*, December; publication of *The American Language* (Third Edition).

1924 First issue of the *American Mercury*, with Mencken and Nathan as co-editors, appears in January; covers Republican National Convention, Cleveland, June; covers Democratic National Convention, New York City, June; begins column for the *Chicago Tribune*, November 9 (column continues until 29 January 1928); publication of *Prejudices: Fourth Series*.

1925 Nathan withdraws as co-editor of the *American Mercury*, February; Mencken covers the trial of John Scopes in Dayton, Tennessee, July (arguably Mencken's finest writing as a journalist); death of mother, Anna Abhau Mencken, December 13; publication of *Americana, 1925*.

1926 *American Mercury* is banned in Boston because of "Hatrack," April; publication of *Notes on Democracy*, *Prejudices: Fifth Series*, and *Americana, 1926*.

1927 Publication of *Prejudices: Sixth Series* and *Selected Prejudices*.

1928 Covers Pan American Conference, Havana, January; covers Republican National Convention, Kansas City, June; covers Democratic National Convention, Houston, June; Knopf publishes *Menckeniana: A Schimpflexikon* (a collection of abuse heaped upon Mencken).

1930 Covers London Naval Conference, January–February; marries Sara Powell Haardt in Baltimore, August 27, and couple sets up residence at 704 Cathedral Street, Baltimore; publication of *Treatise on the Gods*; begins diary (published as *The Diary of H. L. Mencken*, 1989).

1931 Maryland's Eastern Shore erupts after Mencken writes
newspaper columns attacking lynching there, December.

1932 Covers Republican National Convention, Chicago, June;
covers Democratic National Convention, Chicago,
June–July; *Making a President* published.

1933 Eastern Shore erupts after Mencken attacks lynching again,
October; Mencken resigns as editor of the *American
Mercury*, December.

1934 Writes first column for the New York *American*, July 9
(final column appears on 22 April 1936); delivers speech to
the Gridiron Club in Washington, D.C., December 8, highly
publicized controversy with President Franklin Roosevelt;
publication of *Treatise on Right and Wrong*.

1935 Sara Haardt Mencken dies of tubercular meningitis,
Baltimore, May 31.

1936 Leaves 704 Cathedral Street and returns to 1524 Hollins
Street, March; the *New Yorker* publishes the first of the
sketches later used in the *Days* trilogy, April 11; covers
Republican National Convention, Cleveland, June; covers
Democratic National Convention, Philadelphia, June;
covers Townsend Convention, Cleveland, July; covers
Coughlin Convention, Cleveland, August; publication of
The American Language (Fourth Edition).

1937 Publication of *The Sunpapers of Baltimore*, written with
Frank R. Kent, Gerald W. Johnson, and Hamilton Owens.

1938 Serves as temporary editor of the Baltimore *Evening Sun*,
February–May; begins "Sunday Articles" for Baltimore
Sun, May 16 (column continues until 2 February 1941);
travels alone in Germany, June–July.

1939 Suffers minor stroke, "generalized arteriosclerosis," July.

1940 Covers Republican National Convention, Philadelphia,
June; covers Democratic National Convention, Chicago,

July; publication of *Happy Days: 1880–1892,* the first
volume of the autobiographical trilogy.

1941 Stops writing for the *Sunpapers* because of disagreement
concerning President Franklin Roosevelt's foreign policy,
February; begins writing "Thirty-Five Years of Newspaper
Work" (published under the title *Thirty-Five Years of
Newspaper Work: A Memoir by H. L. Mencken,* 1994);
publication of *Heathen Days: 1899–1906.*

1942 Begins "My Life as Author and Editor" (published under
the same title, 1993); publication of *A New Dictionary of
Quotations.*

1943 Publication of *Heathen Days: 1890–1936.*

1945 Publication of *The American Language*: *Supplement I.*

1946 Publication of *Christmas Story.*

1947 Suffers minor stroke, August; publication of *The Days of
H. L. Mencken,* a one-volume edition of the
autobiographical trilogy.

1948 Rejoins the staff of the *Sunpapers,* June; covers Republican
National Convention, Philadelphia, June; covers
Democratic National Convention, Philadelphia, July; covers
Progressive Party Convention, Philadelphia, July; writes
sixteen columns for the Baltimore *Sun,* the last an attack on
segregation, August 1–November 9; suffers stroke that robs
him of his ability to read and write, November 23;
publication of *The American Language: Supplement II.*

1949 Publication of *A Mencken Chrestomathy.*

1955 Publication of *The Vintage Mencken,* edited by Alistair
Cooke.

1956 Dies in his sleep of a coronary occlusion, January 29;
posthumous publication of *Minority Report: H. L.
Mencken's Notebooks.*

Author's note: This chronology is more detailed than the one that appears in the 1989 Continuum edition. In constructing this chronology, I have drawn upon the chronology put together for *Thirty-Five Years of Newspaper Work: A Memoir by H. L. Mencken*, editors Fred Hobson, Vincent Fitzpatrick, and Bradford Jacobs (Baltimore: Johns Hopkins University Press, 1994), xxvii–xxxii.

1906, Mencken at age 26. Photograph by Meredith Janvier. (Courtesy Enoch Pratt Free Library)

1913, Mencken at age 33 in the office of the Baltimore *Sun*. (Courtesy Enoch Pratt Free Library)

1927, The famous portrait painted by Nikol Schattenstein when Mencken was 47. His body exudes energy, the energy that gave so much gusto to his prose. He was then at the height of his notoriety during a decade when he was called the most powerful private citizen in America. (Courtesy Enoch Pratt Free Library)

1928, Mencken reads in the parlor at 1524 Hollins Street. F. Scott Fitzgerald visited this room, as did Theodore Dreiser. The secretary to the left of the fireplace holds the copy of *The Adventures of Huckleberry Finn* that so enthralled Mencken as a child. Photograph by Edgar T. Schaefer. (Courtesy Enoch Pratt Free Library)

1929, Mencken joins the neighborhood children in the alley behind 1524 Hollins Street. This alley was, and still is, called Booth Street. This writer, who terrified some opponents and infuriated others, bought candy for the neighborhood kids. (Courtesy Enoch Pratt Free Library)

August 27, 1930, the wedding of Mencken and Sara Powell Haardt at the Episcopal Church of Saint Stephen the Martyr, West Baltimore. Photograph by a *Sun* photographer. (Courtesy Enoch Pratt Free Library)

1930, Mencken and Clarence Darrow at 704 Cathedral Street, Baltimore. This lithograph of a brewery was one of Mencken's favorite possessions. (Courtesy Enoch Pratt Free Library)

1933, Mencken the
radio "crooner."
Photograph by Ray
Lee Jackson.
(Courtesy Enoch
Pratt Free Library)

1933, Mencken enjoys a cold beer at the Rennert Hotel, Baltimore right
after the repeal of Prohibition. The hatless man to Mencken's left is
Hamilton Owens, the distinguished author, editor and journalist.
(Courtesy Enoch Pratt Free Library)

1936, Mencken loved covering the presidential conventions, the gaudy spectacle of American democracy in the flesh. Here, he covers the Republican Convention in Cleveland that nominated Governor Alf Landon in June, 1936. Mencken befriended Landon and later gave a dinner for him in Baltimore. (Courtesy Enoch Pratt Free Library)

CHAPTER 1

The Bourgeois Baltimorean

I, unfortunately, did not come up from that log cabin.
My misfortune was that my father was relatively well-off.
It has been a curse to me all my life. Nobody will believe
me on that ground. It seems to be the idea in America that
no man is worth listening to unless he has had some
experience in sweat shops.
—*H. L. Mencken Speaks (Caedmon Records)*

"I am by nature the most orderly of mortals," Mencken saw fit to
inform his reading public. "I have a place for every article of my
personal property, whether a bible or a cocktail shaker.... I am
never late for trains. I never run short of collars. I never go out
with a purple necktie on a blue shirt. I never fail to appear in time
for dinner without telephoning or telegraphing."[1] Mencken's
career was characterized by permanence rather than instability, by
decorum within society rather than querulous isolation from it, by
solvency rather than indebtedness. Such values marked Mencken's
life as much as his distinctive style marked his writing.

As a citizen, Mencken remained accessible; as a writer, he
proved a successful businessman. Although he saw the telephone
more as an intrusion than a convenience, he kept one with a listed
number. He answered all his mail, almost invariably on the day

---

[1]Mencken, "Reflections on Monogamy," in *Prejudices: Fourth Series*
(New York: Knopf, 1924) 121.

that it arrived. He found nothing commendable in this—it was merely common courtesy—and he took the time to write well over 100,000 letters.[2] Fortunately, Mencken was never troubled by an issue that has plagued a number of other American authors: How is the writer to make a living? No Herman Melville toiling in the obscurity of a custom house, no William Faulkner laboring unhappily as a postal clerk in Mississippi and later as a scriptwriter in Hollywood, Mencken found it easy to make and save money in America. He never conducted a lecture tour and, to the bewilderment of some of his fellow authors, refused to accept an advance on a book. Cautious and perceptive in financial matters—his estate totaled about $300,000, a princely sum in 1956—Mencken was, in this way and others, his father's son. Unfailingly bourgeois in his personal values, Mencken happily researched his ancestry, wrote about it at considerable length for an early biographer, and never turned on the class that begot him.[3]

Prominent in Germany, the Menckens also prospered in America. One of Mencken's ancestors bore Prince Otto von Bismarck, the first chancellor of the German empire. But in 1848, a year of revolution, Mencken's paternal grandfather, Burkhardt Ludwig Mencken, emigrated to America in order "to escape a threatened overdose" of democracy.[4] Burkhardt married three years later, and his first son, August, was born in Baltimore in 1854. In 1875, with thirty-five dollars in capital, August and his

---

[2]Carl Bode, "Sincerely, H.L.M." in *The New Mencken Letters*, ed. Carl Bode (New York: Dial Press, 1977) 3. Previously undiscovered Mencken letters, held in private hands, are coming to light with considerable frequency. His output as a correspondent is staggering.

[3]"$300,000 Estate Left by Mencken," *New York Times*, 15 February 1956. For Isaac Goldberg's *The Man Mencken: A Biographical and Critical Survey* (New York: Simon and Schuster, 1925) Mencken wrote "Autobiographical Notes, 1925." This volume and "Autobiographical and Critical Notes, 1941" are valuable sources of information about Mencken's life and opinions. These volumes are housed in the Mencken Collection at the Enoch Pratt Free Library in Baltimore (henceforth designated "EPFL").

[4]Mencken, *Happy Days: 1880–1892* (New York: Knopf, 1940) 92.

brother Henry established a successful cigar factory. While he paid good wages, August was a high-tariff Republican who declined to run a union shop. An infidel incapable of taking religion seriously, August despised all reform movements and believed that the conduct of one's neighbors was best left alone.[5] All of these matters—the business acumen, political conservatism, agnosticism, contempt for reform, and insistence upon personal freedom—would be passed on to August's eldest son. In late 1879, August married Anna Margaret Abhau, another first-generation German-American. In September 1880, Henry Louis was born "with no more public spirit than a cat."[6]

In 1883, the Menckens moved to 1524 Hollins Street. A typical Baltimore row house, this three-story building with the red-brick front and white-marble steps would become one of the most famous literary addresses in America. With the exception of the nearly six years during and right after his marriage, Mencken would live here for the rest of his life. Unpretentious, efficient, comfortable, the house stood as the objective correlative of the family's way of living, a style that its most famous son would do his best to continue. Acutely interested in his heritage, Mencken would remark years later that the essence of a home "lies in its

---

[5]Mencken's ancestry is covered, in varying degrees, in the biographies. Goldberg's discussion in *The Man* Mencken of this issue is extensive. The other book that appeared in 1925, Ernest Boyd's *H. L. Mencken* (New York: McBride), is much briefer. Two more biographies appeared during Mencken's lifetime: William Manchester's *Disturber of the Peace: The Life of H. L. Mencken* (New York: Harper, 1950) and Edgar Kemler's *The Irreverent Mr. Mencken* (Boston: Little, Brown, 1950). Carl Bode's *Mencken* (Carbondale IL: Southern Illinois University Press, 1969); Fred Hobson's *Mencken: A Life* (New York: Random House, 1994), and Terry Teachor's *The Skeptic: A Live of H.L. Mencken* (New York: Harper Rollins, 2002), examine Mencken's life in considerable detail. Douglas C. Stenerson's *H. L. Mencken: Iconoclast from Baltimore* (Chicago: University of Chicago Press, 1971) and Charles A. Fecher's *Mencken: A Study of His Thought* (New York: Knopf, 1978) are primarily critical studies, both quite valuable, that offer biographical information as well.

[6]Mencken, *Newspaper Days: 1899–1906* (New York: Knopf, 1941) vii.

permanence, in its capacity for accretion and solidification, in its quality of representing, in all its details, the personalities of the people who live in it."[7] Like Proust and Faulkner, Mencken never doubted the influence of time past upon time present. The narrow back yard extended half a city block. Union Square Park lay right across the street, and open country beckoned only a few blocks to the west. Mencken's uncle lived next door, a grandfather only a few blocks away. There was enough money for servants and summer houses. "My early life was placid, serene, uneventful, and happy," Mencken recalled. He and his siblings, two brothers and a sister, "were encapsulated in affection and kept fat, saucy, and contented."[8] Mencken read his first story at seven, delighted in the small printing press that he received during his eighth year, and devoured *Huckleberry Finn* at nine—"probably the most stupendous event of my life," he declared.[9]

Mencken's formal education began in September 1886 at F. Knapp's Institute in downtown Baltimore, a private elementary school with many pupils of German heritage. In 1892, he entered the Baltimore Polytechnic Institute, a public high school, and graduated in 1896, a fifteen-year-old valedictorian. He never went to school again—no Mencken male in America ever attended college—and missed few opportunities to disparage the higher education that he had spurned. He could be caustic: "I was...spared the intellectual humiliations of a college education." Or he could draw upon his considerable skill as an ironist and guffaw, "Some boys go to college and succeed in getting out.

---

[7]Mencken, "On Living in Baltimore," Baltimore *Evening Sun*, 16 February 1925. See "On Living in Baltimore," in *Prejudices: Fifth Series* (New York: Knopf, 1926) 237–43. For further discussion of the influence of Baltimore in general and 1524 Hollins Street in particular, see Stenerson, *H. L. Mencken: Iconoclast from Baltimore*, 34–66; Stenerson, "Baltimore: Source and Sustainer of Mencken's Values," *Menckeniana* 41 (Spring 1972): 1–9; Fecher, *Mencken: A Study of His Thought* (New York: Knopf, 1978) 23–80; and Frank R. Shivers, *Maryland Wits & Baltimore Bards* (Baltimore: Maclay, 1985) 161–86.

[8]Mencken, *Happy Days*, vii.

[9]Ibid., 163.

Others go to college and never succeed in getting out. The latter are called professors."[10] The professors, not surprisingly, fired back, and Mencken's battles with the academy were highly entertaining.

The next two and one-half years marked the bleakest period in Mencken's life. He wanted to learn to write professionally, but August Mencken expected his oldest son to join the family business. Mencken refused to disobey and worked as both a cigar maker and a salesman. He grew so despondent that he considered suicide.[11]

On January 13, 1899, August Mencken died of kidney failure. Now the head of the household, Henry Louis continued at the cigar factory by day. Every evening for four weeks, he presented himself at the Baltimore *Herald*. Finally, he was given an unpaid assignment, and on February 24 the *Herald* ran the following news item: "A horse, a buggy and several sets of harness, valued in all at about $250, were stolen last night from the stable of Howard Quinlan, near Kingsville. The county police are at work on the case, but so far no trace of either thieves or booty has been found." The editor only grunted at Mencken's copy, and no one else told the young reporter: "I greet you at the beginning of a great career." In June, Mencken went on salary, seven dollars per week, and never looked back. At age eighteen, his vocation and avocation were one, and Mencken delighted in the "maddest, gladdest, damndest existence ever enjoyed by mortal youth."[12]

Mencken's abilities as a journalist quickly became apparent. He rose from reporter to drama critic in 1901; that same year, he was appointed editor of the *Sunday Herald*. By 1903, he was serving as city editor of the morning paper. The next year,

---

[10]Mencken, "Under the Elms," in *A Mencken Chrestomathy* (New York: Knopf, 1949) 132–33; Mencken, "Répétition Générale," *Smart Set* 71 (June 1923): 39.

[11]Mencken, "Notes and Additions to *Newspaper Days*," EPFL. Quoted by Shivers, *Maryland Wits & Baltimore Bards*, 179.

[12]Mencken, *Newspaper Days* 7, 8, ix.

Mencken, by his own account, became a man. The Baltimore fire, one of the major American conflagrations, began on February 7, 1904. The *Herald* building blazed, and the homeless staff struggled to get out a paper in Baltimore, Washington, and Philadelphia. Mencken did not get home for a week. He went into the fire "a boy," fueled by "the hot gas of youth," and emerged "almost a middle-aged man, spavined by responsibility and aching in every sinew."[13]

During the year in which the fire literally changed the face of Baltimore, the establishment of the Saturday Night Club added to the continuity of Mencken's life. Music was always Mencken's first love; he wrote about it whenever he had the chance and delighted in playing the piano. For nearly half a century the club was marked by diversity; newspapermen played here, as did professors, physicians, and professional musicians. The music began promptly at 8 P.M., lasted two hours, and was followed by beer, hearty food, and conversation that ranged from the earthy to the erudite. For a man who so actively spurned membership in organizations—Mencken never tired of lampooning the joiner—his continuing participation in the Saturday Night Club demonstrated his respect for tradition, good friends, and what he saw as the greatest of the art forms.[14]

Although the *Herald* struggled after the fire, Mencken's ascent continued. In 1905, he was appointed managing editor. The next year he became editor-in-chief, perhaps the youngest in America. After the *Herald* folded in 1906, Mencken turned down an offer from the *New York Times* and joined the Baltimore *Evening News*, where he stayed about six weeks. He then signed

---

[13]Ibid., 278.

[14]The best discussion of this subject is *H. L. Mencken on Music*, ed. Louis Cheslock (New York: Knopf, 1961). Dr. Cheslock's postlude gives the history of the Saturday Night Club. More of Dr. Cheslock's writing on the club appears in *Menckeniana*: 83 (Fall 1982): 13–16; 84 (Winter 1982): 13–16; 94 (Summer 1985): 1–9; 95 (Fall 1985): 11–16; 96 (Winter 1985): 6–9; and 97 (Spring 1986): 8–13.

on with the Baltimore *Sun*, an association that would endure more than forty years. His copy was quickly noticed. "Think of it!" exclaimed Colonel Henry Watterson of the Louisville *Courier-Journal*. "The staid old *Baltimore Sun* has got itself a real Whangdoodle."[15]

It is easy to picture this Whangdoodle in his middle twenties: buoyant in his chunky build (about 5'8" and 175 pounds), the brown hair slicked down and parted in the middle, a cigar jutting from his mouth at a rakish angle, and a perpetually impish gleam in his light blue eyes. The world seemed full of fun; Mencken was young, not easily impressed, and eager to make contacts outside of Baltimore. In one of his more appealing letters, the novelist and magazine editor Theodore Dreiser described his first meeting with Mencken in New York City in 1908:

> With the sang-froid of a Caesar or a Napoleon [Mencken] made himself comfortable in a large and impressive chair which was designed primarily to reduce the over-confidence of the average beginner. And from that particular and unintended vantage point he beamed on me with the confidence of a smirking fox about to devour a chicken.... I began to laugh. "Well, well," I said, "if it isn't Anheuser's own brightest boy out to see the town." And with that unfailing readiness for nonsensical fight that has always characterized him, he proceeded to insist that this was true. Certainly he *was* Baltimore's richest brewer's son and the yellow shoes and bright tie that he was wearing were characteristic of the jack-dandies and rowdy-dows of his native town. Why not[?] What else did I expect? His father brewed the best beer in the world.[16]

---

[15]Colonel Henry Watterson, editorial, Louisville *Courier-Journal*, 25 August 1906.

[16]Theodore Dreiser to Dr. Isaac Goldberg, 24 August 1925, in Goldberg, *The Man Mencken*, 379–80.

Dreiser was sufficiently impressed to secure for the Baltimorean, without Mencken's knowing it, a position as book reviewer for the *Smart Set*, a literary monthly magazine published in New York City. Mencken thereby acquired his first national forum. Moreover, it was through the *Smart Set* that he met George Jean Nathan, the distinguished drama critic from Indiana, two years Mencken's junior. In time, the two would frolic as one of America's more memorable vaudeville acts.[17]

In 1910, Mencken helped to establish the Baltimore *Evening Sun*. In 1913, he met Alfred A. Knopf, the publisher with whom he would establish a long, friendly, and mutually beneficial relationship. In October 1914, Mencken and Nathan were promoted to co-editors of the *Smart Set*. Clearly, these early years proved kind to the Baltimorean. Mencken was indeed, as Dreiser colorfully stated, "Anheuser's own brightest boy": congenial, talented, industrious—and also, like Dreiser, a German-American.

The "shot heard round the world" echoed loudly on Hollins Street. Gabriel Princip, a Serbian nationalist proclaiming liberty, assassinated the Austrian Archduke Franz Ferdinand at Sarajevo. For Mencken, Dreiser, and other Americans of German heritage, Princip declared nothing of the sort. The onset of World War I ended the era of good feeling between Mencken and America. He would continue to laugh at his native land, continue to revel in its excesses, but he would never again view it with innocence.

Two generations removed from Europe, Mencken could read German but could not write it well. While he could understand most of what was said to him, he could not speak the language fluently. He recognized that a German victory in Europe would not benefit him at all and that a German victory over America would damage him greatly. He did not, he emphasized, want to

---

[17]Carleton Jones, "Living with Brickbats, But Loving Bouquets," Baltimore *Sun*, 12 October 1980.

serve as a spokesperson for the German cause.[18] Mencken did, however, have a sentimental attachment to the land of his ancestors. The hearty ambiance of German life—its beer, food, and music—appealed to him, and, as a strident Anglophobe, Mencken bore no positive feeling for England as the mother country. "England gave us Puritanism," he remarked acidly; "Germany gave us Pilsner. Take your choice." Moreover, once the war began in August 1914, Mencken quickly saw what many of his fellow citizens either failed to recognize or refused to acknowledge: that the pro-British press colored the news, that America's professed neutrality was bogus.[19]

Mencken used his "Free Lance" column in the *Evening Sun* to present the side of the opposition. "The moral implications of the war begin to clarify," he bludgeoned his readers on August 5. "It was immoral for Germany to go to the aid of Austria, but it was perfectly moral for France to go to the aid of Russia and for England to go to the aid of France.... It is a proof of noble sentiment for England to threaten Germany from the rear, but it is an indication of natural vileness for Germany to face three first-class powers from the front." After the *Lusitania* was sunk in 1915, moral indignation grew, but Mencken insisted that, because the ship was an armed vessel carrying munitions, the Germans were not culpable.[20] Not surprisingly, Mencken's attitudes

---

[18]Mencken, "Autobiographical Notes, 1925," 150, EPFL. Mencken to Ellery Sedgwick, 22 May [1915], in *Letters of H. L. Mencken*, ed. Guy J. Forgue (New York: Knopf, 1961) 72. Mencken to Fielding Hudson Garrison, 30 August 1918, in Forgue, *Letters*, 128.

[19]Mencken, "The Free Lance," Baltimore *Evening Sun*, 31 December 1914. See Markus F. Motsch, "H. L. Mencken and German Kultur," *German-American Studies* 6 (Fall 1973): 21–42. For discussions of Mencken and World War I, see especially Stenerson, *H. L. Mencken: Iconoclast from Baltimore*, 165–183; and Merritt W. Moseley, Jr., "H. L. Mencken and the First World War," *Menckeniana* 56 (Summer 1976): 8–15.

[20]Mencken, "The Free Lance," Baltimore *Evening Sun*, 8 May 1915. See Stenerson, *H. L. Mencken: Iconoclast from Baltimore*, 173–74; and Bode, *Mencken*, 112.

alienated a number of his readers as well as the management of the *Sunpapers*, which supported England. In October 1915, Mencken was forced to give up the "Free Lance" after four and one-half successful years. He did not step down quietly. "The truth that survives," he remarked contemptuously in his penultimate column, "is the lie that is pleasantest to believe."[21]

Clearly, Mencken had assumed an adversarial position with his employer. Uncertain as to what else to do, the *Sunpapers* sent Mencken abroad as a war correspondent and warned its readers not to expect unbiased reporting. After covering the eastern front, Mencken withdrew in February 1917 when America broke off relations with Germany. He returned in March, the month prior to America's entry into the war.[22]

He found America no more attractive than he had before he went abroad. Some of the developments, mere annoyances, were caused by what Mencken saw as the pettiness of the Anglo-Saxon mentality. For example, names of streets and foods were changed; Baltimore's German Street was rechristened Redwood Street, and sauerkraut masqueraded as "liberty cabbage." Other developments proved far more serious. Mencken had already lost one column in the *Evening Sun*, and he lost another with the New York *Evening Mail* when its publisher was unjustly accused of receiving financial aid from Germany. Moreover, Mencken's mail was opened *en route* to Hollins Street, and, fearing for the safety of his mother and sister in the face of mob violence, he hesitated to leave Baltimore. Mencken concluded that the United States had rescinded the civil liberties of its German-American citizens. The

---

[21]Mencken, "The Free Lance," Baltimore *Evening Sun*, 23 October 1915.

[22]See Bode, *Mencken*, 113; and Moseley, "H. L. Mencken and the First World War," 10. Mencken, "Berlin, February, 1917," ed. Richard J. Schrader and Vincent Fitzpatrick, in *Dictionary of Literary Biography Yearbook, 2000*, ed. Matthew J. Bruccoli (Detroit: The Gale Group, 2001) 195–213.

time was coming, he remarked, when those with names like his
would be jailed.[23]
      In the end, the vicious attacks upon Mencken's writing were
not what bothered him. He understood, as all professional writers
should, that his adversaries had the right to criticize his work as
they pleased. Certainly, he was unhappy with some of the libelous
statements made about him—that he was, for example, "a former
subject" of the kaiser—but he never sued.[24] This was not his way.
What bothered Mencken most of all was the lack of fair play, what
he later called "the savage persecution of all opponents and critics
of the war...the complete abandonment of all decency, decorum
and self-respect."[25] Messianic in its delusions about democracy
and saving the world, America at this time was governed by no
mere mortal but by "Archangel Woodrow," a figure "utterly
without honor" and a "damned liar."[26] Mencken rarely attacked an
opponent incapable of fighting back. During the war, however,
Mencken was like a boxer led shackled into the ring and forced to
lead with his chin. The jingoistic critics— "star-spangled men," he
dubbed them—merely wrapped themselves in the flag, and free
exchange ceased.[27] Mencken grew so disgusted that he considered
leaving American permanently.
      He endured, however, and when the tumult was over, he
recognized that World War I had actually helped his career.[28]

---

[23]Mencken to Theodore Dreiser, [March or early April 1917], in *Dreiser-Mencken Letters: The Correspondence of Theodore Dreiser and H. L. Mencken, 1907–1945*, 2 volumes, ed Thomas P. Riggio (Philadelphia: University of Pennsylvania Press) 295–96; Mencken to Louis Untermeyer, [late July 1917], in Forgue, *Letters*, 108–109.

[24]Mencken, *Menckeniana: A Schimpflexikon* (New York: Knopf, 1928) 53.

[25]Mencken, "On Being an American," in *Prejudices: Third Series* (New York: Knopf 1922) 46.

[26]Mencken, "The Archangel Woodrow," in *A Mencken Chrestomathy*, 248–51. Mencken to Burton Rascoe, [summer 1920?], in Forgue, *Letters*, 188.

[27]Mencken, "Star-Spangled Men," in *A Mencken Chrestomathy*, 597–606.

[28]Mencken to Fielding Hudson Garrison, 17 November 1919, in Forgue, *Letters*, 161.

Freed for a while from the strictures of daily journalism, Mencken had the opportunity to write several successful books that he might not otherwise have undertaken. Moreover, after the debacle at Versailles, when more Americans cast a cold eye upon President Wilson's grandiloquence, the country was more receptive to what Mencken had to say. While World War I marked the most important event in Mencken's young adulthood, middle age was beckoning, and he welcomed the change. Mencken turned forty in 1920, and America during the coming decade would regale him more than it ever had previously. When the expatriates fled to Europe, he would watch the boats sail and have a delightful time lampooning the culture that they found so unconducive to art. He would cover the trial of a high-school science teacher and football coach who, more than sixty years after the publication of Charles Darwin's *Origin of Species*, was arrested for teaching the theory of evolution, the trial at which a man nominated three times for the presidency of the United States thundered that man is not a mammal. "This is far worse than anything you could imagine, even under the bowl [that is, when inebriated], Mencken would laughingly correspond with a friend back in Baltimore. "Every last scoundrel in sight is a Christian, including the town Jew. No wonder the Romans finally bumped off the son of Joseph."[29] Only in America could Mencken have found for himself such a place in the sun.

The 1920s marked the zenith of Mencken's career. The Baltimorean was, as Walter Lippmann remarked in 1926, "the most powerful personal influence upon this whole generation of educated people."[30] While Mencken's writing elicited considerable commentary, his personal life generated frequent and colorful copy. In Mencken's view, a man cavorted most knavishly in his

---

[29]Mencken to Raymond Pearl, [14? July 1925], in Bode, *The New Mencken Letters* (New York: Dial Press, 1977) 187–88.
[30]Walter Lippmann, "H. L. Mencken," *Saturday Review of Literature* 3 (11 December 1926): 413–14.

forties. After the death of the movie star Rudolph Valentino, Mencken suggested waggishly that he might become the sheik's successor.[31] Mencken's one domestic tour became almost legendary. In October 1926, he left Baltimore on a railway journey that went first through the Southeast. Mencken took this opportunity to endorse men from several of the states for the presidency. The tour swung through the Southwest and ended in California, that land of palm trees and movie stars that Mencken found particularly garish. Aimee Semple McPherson, the controversial evangelist, claimed Mencken as a convert. Always generous, he reciprocated by nominating her for Miss America.[32]

By 1925, Mencken's finances were such that he could have stopped working. "I believe it is discreditable to be needy," he explained to a correspondent two years later. "Economic independence is the foundation of the only sort of freedom worth a damn." During these boom times, he for the most part resisted the lure of the supposedly easy money to be made in the stock market. When the crash occurred in October 1929, he lost little.[33] Mencken's financial conservatism and continued solvency would definitely color his response to the Depression and President Franklin Roosevelt's New Deal.

For the Baltimorean, the greatest personal catastrophe of this decade was the death of Anna Abhau Mencken on December 13, 1925. The eldest son in an old-fashioned family, Mencken took very seriously his responsibilities to his widowed mother. However, just as August's death in 1899 had freed Mencken to pursue his career in journalism, so did Anna's death allow Mencken to consider marriage more seriously than he had before.

---

[31]Sara Mayfield, *The Constant Circle: H. L. Mencken and His Friends* (New York: Delacorte Press, 1968) 60.

[32]Ibid., 107.

[33]Mencken, "Autobiographical Notes, 1925," 115, EPFL. The quoted remark is from Mencken to Charles Green Shaw, 2 December 1927 in Forgue, *Letters,* 307. Mencken discussed his small losses in a letter to Herbert Parrish, 6 November 1929 (Princeton University).

He had, in fact, already met his bride-to-be. In 1923, one of America's most outspoken bachelors—the man who boasted, "If I ever marry, it will be on a sudden impulse, as a man shoots himself"—had lectured at Goucher College. His subject was ostensibly "The Trade of Letters," but he turned instead to a subject that he found more amusing, "How to Catch a Husband."[34] He met Sara Powell Haardt, Goucher's youngest faculty member and an aspiring writer from Montgomery, Alabama, who was eighteen years his junior. Mencken and Sara embarked upon what he would recall gratefully as a "beautiful adventure."[35]

Their courtship sometimes bumped along. Sara was put off, at times, by the highly publicized rumors of Mencken's involvement with other women; the tabloids had him marrying a Hollywood star and an opera singer. Moreover, the couple spent considerable time apart—with Mencken's travel abroad, his coverage of the presidential conventions, his frequent trips to New York City to edit the *Smart Set* and the *American Mercury*, and Sara's sojourn in Hollywood in 1927 as a script writer. Sara's poor health, however, proved the most disruptive factor. Tubercular, she was confined to a sanitarium in Maryland throughout 1924, and she spent all of the following year and part of 1926 in Alabama. But Mencken kept calling, attracted by her ability as a writer—she was quiet while he was loud—her charm, her courage in the face of illness, perhaps above all by the sense of humor so evident in her ability to laugh at him. Sara referred to one of America's most famous men as the "Palm of Learning" and perhaps because

---

[34]Mencken to Charles Green Shaw, 2 December 1927, in Forgue, *Letters,* 306. For more detailed discussions of the courtship and marriage, see Marion Elizabeth Rodgers, introduction in *Mencken and Sara, A Life in Letters: The Intimate Correspondence of H. L. Mencken and Sara Haardt* (New York: McGraw-Hill, 1987) 1–73; Anne Henley, introduction in *Southern Souvenirs: Selected Stories and Essays of Sara Haardt* (Tuscaloosa: University of Alabama Press, 1999) 1–45; Bode, *Mencken,* 279–303; Mayfield, *The Constant Circle,* 131–213; and Hobson, *Mencken: A Life,* 295–356.

[35]Mencken to Ellery Sedgwick, 7 June [1935], in Forgue, *Letters,* 392.

Mencken glistened during those humid Baltimore summers, the "Duke of Palmolive."[36]

They married on August 27, 1930. After a honeymoon trip to Canada, the couple returned to a spacious third-floor apartment at 704 Cathedral Street off Mount Vernon Place, one of Baltimore's oldest and most esteemed neighborhoods. The marriage prospered for nearly five years. Mencken liked his beer and cigars; Sara preferred Coca-Cola. Her taste ran to the Victorian, but one of Mencken's favorite possessions, a huge lithograph of a brewery, hung prominently in the dining room. Both Mencken and Sara were old enough, and sensible enough, not to try to change one another. Despite all efforts, however, Sara's health continued to decline, and she died from tubercular meningitis on May 31, 1935. She was thirty-seven. "Now I feel completely dashed and dismayed," the usually stoical Mencken lamented. "What a cruel and idiotic universe we live in!"[37] Mencken tried to live alone in the apartment but found too many ghosts. He returned permanently to Hollins Street in March 1936.

What he found outside his door in no way allayed his personal grief. During the 1930s, as during those difficult times brought by World War I, Mencken came to feel like an alien in America. His response to the Depression infuriated a number of his contemporaries who saw him, at best, as a corporate man, at worst as a callous and unenlightened reactionary writing nonsense. In 1932, Mencken was elected to the Board of Directors of Alfred A. Knopf, Inc.; two years later, he joined the Board of Directors of the Baltimore *Sunpapers*. While Mencken's book royalties dropped during the Depression, he was still able to live comfortably. As much of America slid to the Left politically and sided with the proletariat, Mencken lined up squarely with the bourgeoisie. Quite simply, he refused to turn on the class that had begotten him.

---

[36]Bode, *Mencken*, 282.
[37]Mencken to Ellery Sedgwick, 7 June [1935], *In Forgue* 392.

It bears noting here, however, that Mencken the author and
Mencken the man differed appreciably. Mencken the writer could
only look back upon what he saw as a more praiseworthy
American past—a time of competence, self-reliance, and more
personal freedom—and compare it to the present monolithic age
that he depicted through such a caustic image as myriads of
nameless faces snouting and grunting and gorging at the public
troughs. But while Mencken the public figure could only deplore
what he saw happening to the traditional American work ethic,
Mencken the private citizen felt a good deal of sympathy for those
broken by hard times. During 1932, for example, when he saw the
breadlines in Times Square, the profoundly shocked Mencken was
rendered speechless. After Mencken returned to Baltimore, a
transient appeared at the offices of the *American Mercury*. He
wanted to thank the stranger who had first offered encouragement
and had then taken off his overcoat and given it away. The
overcoat was Mencken's.[38] The public saw only Mencken the
tiger, not Mencken the lamb.

During this decade of personal loss and public disapproval,
hard work provided Mencken's salvation. Among other projects,
he edited and wrote the preface for *Southern Album*, a posthumous
collection of Sara's short stories. He contributed a number of
chapters to *The Sunpapers of Baltimore* and wrote, for the
newspaper, an eighteen-part study of the University of Maryland
and an even longer series on the Johns Hopkins Hospital. He even
edited the *Evening Sun* for three and one-half months in 1938.
Wearing a Princeton beer jacket and carrying a spittoon, Mencken
made his assault upon the composing room. Mencken at fifty-
seven was thinking, perhaps, of the good old days on the *Herald*.[39]

At this point in his career, Mencken confronted an opponent
far stronger and more pernicious than the jingoists of yesterday or
the current radicals. The enemy was time, an opponent that

---

[38]Manchester, *Disturber of the Peace*, 261.
[39]Bode, *Mencken*, 199.

Mencken, like all productive people, feared the most. In July 1939, he suffered a minor stroke. "I begin to smell the breath of angels," he told a correspondent later that year.[40] His health continued to decline during the next decade. But while he worked more slowly—sometimes he could manage only five hundred words per day—he remained productive as an author of books and as a journalist. As individualistic as ever, Mencken put together an anthology of his writing which he insisted upon calling, to the consternation of Alfred A. Knopf, *A Mencken Chrestomathy*. Always wry about the human condition, Mencken wrote the foreword to a collection of pieces abut hanging gathered by his brother August, a volume with the macabre but memorable title of *By the Neck*.

On the evening of November23, 1948, Mencken suffered a serious stroke. Although he survived, the aftereffects were gruesome. Mencken's speech faltered, and his memory failed. He forgot the names of everyday items as well as those of friends whom he had known for decades. Most important, he lost the ability to read and write. Mencken concluded that his mind had been irreparably damaged, and he spoke of 1948 as the year of his death.[41]

The family whom Mencken in good health had served so faithfully now reciprocated. August Mencken, an engineer, retired to devote full time to his brother's care. Previously, an established routine had helped to make Mencken remarkably productive as a writer. Now, a different sort of routine made it possible for this craftsman, cruelly deprived of his tools, to make it through the day. William Manchester came to read Mencken the newspaper; George Jean Nathan telephoned faithfully, and Alfred A. Knopf

---

[40]Mencken to Jim Tully, 3 November 1939, in Forgue, *Letters*, 440. See Bode, *Mencken*, 367–68.
[41]Bode, *Mencken*, 372. James T. Farrell, "Notes Addressed to a Man Among the Angels," *Menckeniana* 18 (Summer 1966): 1–2.

was boundlessly generous.[42] Mencken found television moronic, but he attended an occasional movie and still enjoyed listening to music. Most of all, this childless widower liked to watch the children frolic in the square where, the century before, he had gamboled as a young boy. Mencken's life ran full circle. The man who had censured presidents and shaken the literary establishment now dictated his final letter to a young girl who had sent him candy.[43] On January 29, 1956, about twenty weeks past his seventy-fifth birthday, Mencken died in his sleep of a coronary occlusion. This marked the end of a long, tumultuous, and highly publicized journey, but it would be wrong to say that Mencken had finally come home. He had never really left.

Mencken's life was hardly the stuff of legends. He was no Henry David Thoreau isolating himself at Walden Pond; no Ambrose Bierce wandering into the Mexican sunset; no F. Scott Fitzgerald, the golden boy with his storied fall from grace. Mencken lived, instead, as a staunch advocate of the settled middle class. He was fortunate, and he knew it. He remained productive until the night of his stroke. Being alive gave him a fierce joy, a joy evident in the gusto of his prose. Mencken had a love affair with his place of birth and longtime residence; no matter how much more money he could have made elsewhere, Mencken refused to live outside Baltimore. Mencken had few disagreements with his family and could hardly have been more fortunate in his choice of a wife. Despite all the attention heaped upon him, he never took himself too seriously. For half a century, Mencken usually achieved his greatest wish: the opportunity to write as he pleased. In his study on Hollins Street, the autodidact

---

[42]For a discussion of the years after the stroke, see Bode, *Mencken*, 370–75; Hobson, *Mencken: A Life,* 502–34; Robert Allen Durr, "The Last Days of H. L. Mencken," *Yale Review* 48 (August 1958): 58–77; and William Manchester, "The Last Years of H. L. Mencken," *Atlantic* 236 (October 1975): 82–90.

[43]Louis Cheslock, "The Saturday Night Club Diary of Louis Cheslock," (Segment Four) *Menckeniana* 97 (Spring 1986): 10. Mencken to Judy Brilhart, 25 January 1956, in Forgue, *Letters*, 506.

laughed to himself, pecked away at his small Corona, rose several times to wash his hands vigorously—as if some of his subjects were somehow unclean—and produced some of the most accomplished prose nonfiction ever written in America.

CHAPTER 2

Mencken Learns His Trade: 1899-1908

At a time when the respectable bourgeois youngsters of my generation were college freshmen, oppressed by simian sophomores and affronted with balderdash daily by chalky pedagogues, I was at large in a wicked seaport of half a million people, with a front seat at every public show, as free of the night as of the day, and getting earfuls and eyefuls of instruction in a hundred giddy arcana, none of them taught in schools.

–*Mencken,* Newspaper Days *(New York: Knopf, 1941) ix.*

Now it seems so long ago, that fateful day in 1899 when the *Herald* first ran Mencken's copy. William McKinley was president; the horse and buggy outnumbered the automobile; Scott Joplin was making ragtime popular, and Theodore Dreiser had yet to complete *Sister Carrie*. William Faulkner and F. Scott Fitzgerald were children of two and three years, respectively. Now obsolete for a metropolitan daily, the linotype had then revolutionized printing after its patenting thirteen years before. In the city room, editors' blue pencils still danced over foolscap, and the *Herald* had no morgue and only two telephones. Advance men for circuses frequented the newspaper to hawk their shows. And had a frenzied stranger rushed in shouting that he had just met the

Messiah, he might well have been given, along with a sly smile, a batch of copy paper and access to the battered typewriter in the corner. Perhaps he did have a story in him. Things were different then. When Mencken reminisced decades later about the beginning of his career, he spoke, not surprisingly, of "those remote days" and "an era long past and by most persons forgotten."[1]

The young journalist was, by his own account, "goatish and full of an innocent delight in the world." In 1903, on a slow Sunday at the *Herald*, Mencken fabricated a story about a wild man loose in the woods outside Baltimore. Two years later, he concocted an account of the defeat of the Russian fleet by the Japanese, an account that, when the news finally arrived, proved mostly accurate. Mencken collaborated with reporters from other newspapers to synthesize the news. What did it finally matter, he reasoned characteristically, how the stevedore kicked overboard by a mule actually spelled his name? "Life was arduous," Mencken remembered, "but it was gay and carefree. The days chased one another like kittens chasing their tails."[2]

Mencken's productivity and the scope of his journalism show just how arduous these early years were. Between noon and midnight, he sometimes wrote five thousand words of news copy on as many as twelve or fifteen stories, some requiring legwork.[3] He covered city hall, the police stations, and the morgue. He discussed food and drink, music and religion, medicine and fashion. (Nowadays, a journalist might well specialize in one or another of these subjects.) As a drama critic, Mencken received some memorable advice from a managing editor: "The first job of

---

[1] Mencken, *Newspaper Days: 1899–1906* (New York: Knopf, 1941), vi, 167. For a discussion of Mencken's early career, see Carl Bode, "Mencken on His Way," in *The Young Mencken: The Best of His Work* (New York: Dial Press, 1973).

[2] Mencken, *Newspaper Days*, v, x. The incidents described in this paragraph are recounted in chapters 8 and 18.

[3] Ibid., 74

the reviewer is to write a good story—to produce something that people will enjoy reading.... Don't hesitate to use the actors roughly: they are mainly idiots. And don't take a dramatist's pretensions too seriously: he is usually only a showman."[4] In addition to the theater criticism, Mencken churned out poetry for a column entitled "Knocks and Jollies" and short stories that ran under the title "Terse and Terrible Texts." For the weekly feature called "Untold Tales," Mencken wrote buffooneries set in ancient Rome, with characters modeled upon then-current American politicians. Every tale ended with the hanging of the protagonist.[5] In June 1904, the *Herald* sent the young reporter to Chicago to cover the Republican National Convention and, the following month, to St. Louis to capture the Democrats. This spectacle, the gaudy American political system in the flesh, enthralled Mencken, and he would gratefully chronicle seven more sets of conventions over the decades.

In addition to his propensity for laughter, Mencken's early career showed his work ethic, his distrust of purely local celebrity, and his rapidly increasing ability to handle a variety of tasks. Mencken did not disdain hackwork and wrote advertising copy for a fruit company and a cemetery. Mencken even ghosted articles on childcare for a local physician; these were sold to Theodore Dreiser, then editing a woman's magazine. The irony regales to this day: the bachelor journalist discussing pediatrics for a childless, promiscuous novelist suffering though a disastrous marriage. Such nonsense helped to generate one of American literature's most significant friendships.[6] In 1900, Mencken sold

---

[4]Ibid., 111–12
[5]Ibid., 63.
[6]These articles appeared in book form as *What You Ought to Know About Your Baby* by Leonard Keene Hirshberg (New York: Butterick Publishing Company, 1910). They are reprinted in *The H. L. Mencken Baby Book: Comprising the Contents of H. L. Mencken's* What You Ought to Know About Your Baby *with Commentaries,* ed. Howard Markel, M.D. and Frank A. Oski, M.D. (Philadelphia: Hanley & Belfus, Inc., 1990).

his first newspaper piece outside Baltimore and served as the American correspondent for newspapers in Japan, China, and Ceylon. Moreover, he placed poems and short stories in a number of magazines. Mencken's competence was so quickly recognized that, by 1905, he had to submit few unsolicited manuscripts, a heady situation for an author so young.

Ventures into Verse, the first book published under Mencken's name, was issued in 1903. Many of the forty poems in this modest venture of forty pages had appeared previously in the Herald and in various magazines. Ventures into Verse was in part a vanity publication—Mencken paid thirty dollars toward printing costs to a local firm—and only one hundred copies were produced. Twenty-five went out for review; two copies sold.[7] Rudyard Kipling's influence permeates this volume—Mencken later admitted to being a "Kiplingomaniac" in his younger days—and the poems range from the hideous to the respectable.[8] Significantly, a number of the poems show Mencken's handling of ideas that would recur later. Several times, for example, he laughs about the battle of the sexes, an issue that he would discuss at much greater length with In Defense of Women (1918). Later, when Mencken became famous, rumors circulated that he was so embarrassed by Ventures that he bought copies in order to destroy them. Mencken always denied this.[9] Ironically, the field of literature in which Mencken first ventured beyond newspaper and magazine publication marked the genre about which he wrote least perceptively as a critic. Some of his conclusions about poetry are as outlandish as the verses here. After 1903, Mencken never wrote poetry again.

For his next book, Mencken turned to John W. Luce, a publisher in Boston, and to foreign authors. Although Mencken's

---

[7]Mencken, "Autobiographical Notes, 1925," 136–37, EPFL.

[8]Mencken, "The Poet and His Art," in A Mencken Chrestomathy (New York: Knopf, 1949) 453.

[9]Robert F. Nardini, "H. L. Mencken's Ventures into Verse," South Atlantic Quarterly 80 (Spring 1981): 195–205.

later book reviews in the *Smart Set* and the *American Mercury*
focused primarily on American literature, the young critic chose to
write studies of George Bernard Shaw and Friedrich Nietzsche. In
fact, Mencken helped to popularize their writing in America.
Much controversy surrounded the Irishman's plays and the
German's philosophy, and Mencken's decision to discuss such
figures sympathetically reveals his own perspective just as much
as his critical analysis does. Clearly, Mencken felt some affinity
with the playwright whose work had been banned and with the
German who reigned as "the king of all axiom smashers and the
arch dissenter of the age."[10]

George Bernard Shaw: His Plays, which appeared in 1905,
marked Mencken's "first real book" as well as the first book about
Shaw ever printed.[11] After modestly offering this compact study
(130 pages of introduction and text) as a "little handbook,"
Mencken provides plot summaries and rudimentary character
analyses, brief discussion of the previous scholarship, a
biographical sketch, and some comments about the playwright's
essays and novels. Hardly remarkable for its structure or
depth—the book somewhat resembles our current study
guides—*George Bernard Shaw* generally succeeds in its limited
purpose. Mencken's writing, on the other hand, sometimes fails to
please, for the Baltimorean was still, at age twenty-four, searching
for his authentic voice. On occasion, the *Shaw* shows the
rudiments of Mencken's mature style, especially its rollicking
cadences and crackling power. On the other hand, this ingenue
from the literary provinces tries too hard, with thoroughly
predictable results, to write eloquently. A number of allusions
intrude; hyperbole gyrates out of control, and some of the
metaphors are gruesome: *Caesar and Cleopatra*, for example, "has

---

[10]Mencken, *The Philosophy of Friedrich Nietzsche* (Boston: Luce, 1908) ix.
[11]Mencken, *Newspaper Days*, 306. Mencken, "Autobiographical Notes,
1925," 125, 137, EPFL. Quoted by Betty Adler, comp., *H. L. M.: The Mencken
Bibliography* (Baltimore: Johns Hopkins University Press, 1961) 5.

been the football for an immense number of sanguinary critical rushes." When the older Mencken looked back, he was understandably dissatisfied with the prose here.[12]

But far more important than its modest scope and its inconsistent prose, *George Bernard Shaw* shows the similarities between Mencken and his subject. In one of the book's more revealing passages, Mencken enthusiastically traces the influences upon Shaw's work:

> Darwin is dead now, and the public that reads the newspapers remembers him only as the person who first publicly noted the fact that men look a great deal like monkeys. But his soul goes marching on. Thomas Henry Huxley and Herbert Spencer, like a new Ham and a new Shem, spent their lives seeing to that. From him, through Huxley, we have appendicitis, the seedless orange, and our affable indifference to hell. Through Spencer, in like manner, we have...our annual carnivals of catechetical revision, the stampede for church union, and the aforementioned George Bernard Shaw. Each and all of these men and things, it is true, might have appeared if Darwin were yet unborn.... It is possible, certainly, but it is supremely, colossally, and overwhelmingly improbable.

In this lively, highly individualistic account of intellectual history since the publication of *Origin of Species* in 1859, Mencken delineates his own position in the battle between orthodoxy and dissent, the struggle between faith and skepticism. Shaw the iconoclast, then notorious for his discussion of prostitution in *Mrs. Warren's Profession*, clearly attracts Mencken. Always the

---

[12]Mencken, *George Bernard Shaw: His Plays* (Boston: Luce, 1905) vii, 38. Mencken, *Minority Report: H. L. Mencken's Notebooks* (New York: Knopf, 1956) 292.

rationalist, Mencken applauds the mimesis in Shaw's art. Praising the lack of moral purpose in Shaw's writing, Mencken stresses the difference between the playwright and the preacher. Finally, Mencken speaks delightedly of the author who, in *Man and Superman*, makes "a dent in the cosmos with a slapstick."[13] Later when he acquired greater expertise, Mencken would do likewise.

Published in 1908, *The Philosophy of Friedrich Nietzsche* elucidates, even more clearly than the *Shaw*, the nature of Mencken's thought. Moreover, *Nietzsche* shows the Baltimorean's industry, intellectual curiosity, and audacity. Nietzsche had died in 1900, and, at the suggestion of his editor, Mencken undertook an ambitious, 325-page study of the philosopher. Mencken refused to be deterred by his lack of formal training in philosophy and by the fact that he had to struggle through the majority of Nietzsche's voluminous canon, difficult enough in English translation, in the original German.

In this first "complete popular [treatise] upon Nietzsche and his philosophy in English," Mencken sometimes fails in his effort "to translate Nietzsche into terms familiar to everyone."[14] An unwieldy structure mars the book, so do some of Mencken's prose and some of his conclusions. Forced somewhat roughly into three sections of different length (life, art, and influence), the book sometimes wobbles and creaks. (Later, facing an even greater wealth of material with the first edition of *The American Language*, Mencken wrote a graceful study.) As a stylist, Mencken compounds an already difficult subject by writing too abstractly about it. With its overabundance of metaphor, the prose again seems self-conscious, the product of a young writer trying too hard to be literary. Not surprisingly, the older Mencken expressed dissatisfaction with the book.[15] Finally, in his bold

---

[13]Mencken, *Shaw*, 129, 9.
[14]Mencken, "Autobiographical Notes, 1925," 125–6, EPFL. Quoted by Adler, *The Mencken Bibliography*, 5. Mencken, *The Philosophy of Friedrich Nietzsche* (Boston: Luce, 1908) 322–23, ix.
[15]Mencken to Harry L. Wilson, 7 November 1933, in Forgue, *Letters*, 370.

attempt to popularize a complicated subject, Mencken sometimes oversimplifies Nietzsche's ideas. Mencken is guilty, to borrow W. H. A. Williams's apt phrase, of "Darwinizing Nietzsche," of placing the German's ideas too narrowly in the context of the law of natural selection."[16] As is the case with *Shaw*, the reader learns as much about Mencken as about his subject.

With Nietzsche, Mencken discovered a spirit even more kindred than the playwright. With our advantage of hindsight, the biographical similarities seem remarkable: each man's early loss of a father, their hypochondria, and their mental incapacities during their final years. Moreover, Mencken uses for Nietzsche the same "trailblazer" analogy later applied to his own career. Mencken's exegesis of Nietzsche's ideas—in short, the German's gospel according to the Baltimorean—clearly highlights their mutual opponents: altruism, democracy, the gullibility of the masses, and universal manhood suffrage. Mencken draws Nietzsche as an iconoclast stridently endorsing individualism. Ineffectual people, Mencken explains through his subject, use religion to protect themselves from their superiors; an enervating force, religion impedes progress. Life proceeds by the harsh lessons of loss and gain: the strong can succeed only at the expense of the weak. The culture that seeks equality sickens itself, and charity, at best a temporary palliative, ultimately makes the weak even less efficient in the battle life. An advanced culture endorses aristocracy, not of blood or money but rather of intellect and expertise. Perhaps most important, the ideal government has the good sense to leave its private citizens alone. This proclamation would resound throughout Mencken's career.

Beyond argument the most ambitious undertaking of Mencken's early period, *Nietzsche* contains ideas that would be developed with greater facility and certitude.[17] This volume is, in

---

[16]W. H. A. Williams, *H. L. Mencken* (Boston: Hall, 1977) 29. This perceptive discussion continues until page 34.

[17]See Bode, *Mencken*, 82–84.

short, a seminal text for an understanding of Mencken's thought.
For someone familiar with Mencken's mature work, reading
Nietzsche resembles a retrospective viewing of the early films of a
talented but inexperienced young actor, an artist whose presence
would later fill the screen, whose virtuosity would grow so
pronounced that it would expand the possibilities of the craft.
This period from the publication of Mencken's first
newspaper column in 1899 to his appointment in 1908 as a book
reviewer for the *Smart Set* marked the Baltimorean's literary
apprenticeship. His ideas coalesced at this time, and he made no
effort to hide the major influences upon his thought: Darwin,
Herbert Spencer, Thomas Henry Huxley, and Nietzsche. Throughout his career, Mencken would remain a derivative thinker, and his
basic attitudes would change little. For some, this continuity in
Mencken's thought would serve as one of his greatest strengths,
his buttress against the chaos that rocked the twentieth century.
For others, however, Mencken's intellectual stasis, at best obsti-
nate and at worst unenlightened and callous, would prove his bane.
Mencken's prose would change more than his ideas would.
Any portrait of this artist as a young man must acknowledge his
efforts to develop the individualistic style that would distinguish
his work, a style so readily identifiable that his mature prose
would really require no by-line. Critics have disagreed as to when
this mature style first appeared, and Mencken himself made
contradictory statements. Speaking broadly, though, Mencken
asserted that most writers of prose do not mature as stylists until
their thirties.[18] Mencken's own writing from 1910 to 1919, when it

---

[18] Bode points to *Shaw* for the appearance of Mencken's mature style
(*Mencken*, 53), but Kemler speaks of the book about Nietzsche (*The Irreverent
Mr. Mencken*, 30). In "Autobiographical Notes,1925" (EPFL) and
"Autobiographical Notes, 1941," (EPFL) Mencken alternately points to 1905,
1906, and 1907 as years in which his mature style began to manifest itself. In
"Autobiographical Notes, 1925," Mencken makes the generalization that writers
of prose mature during their thirties (125). See Douglas C. Stenerson,

is juxtaposed with these early efforts, more often than not supports this generalization,

Some matters, of course, remained the same. From the beginning, Mencken saw clarity as the hallmark of good prose. Revealingly, he took Thomas Henry Huxley's style, rather than the more Byzantine constructions of, say, a John Ruskin or a Walter Pater, as his model. While they may object stridently to his ideas, Mencken's readers rarely have trouble understanding him. Moreover, this early writing, no matter what the forum, is marked consistently by Mencken's gusto. Young or old, he never doubted that it is better to be wrong than to be boring, a priority that many other critics would see as outlandish.

On the other hand, the writing of this apprenticeship contains a number of devices and strategies that Mencken later used much more proficiently. As an ironist, for example, Mencken would learn that the deft wielding of a scalpel is more destructive, and more entertaining, than a furious assault with an axe. Mencken's vivid analogies, those extended metaphors and similes that he loved to concoct, would change from gaudy appendages to devices woven skillfully into his prose. When they became less ostentatious, the analogies became more effective. Although his early prose can make the reader laugh, Mencken had not yet mastered the timing so crucial to a comic writer. Believing that "a fine ear...is the gauge of all verse, and in fact of all writing," Mencken showed an early interest in the American idiom and imitated George Ade's *Fables in Slang*.[19] Later, Mencken's aural acuity increased to the point that, on occasion, he could write American English that rivals Mark Twain's. Finally, as a young journalist and author of books, Mencken had to adapt to the various levels of diction, as well as the differences in sentence and

---

"Mencken's Early Newspaper Experience: The Genesis of a Style," *American Literature* 37 (May 1965): 153–66.

[19] Mencken to Marcella duPont, 25 June 1938, quoted by Bode, *Mencken*, 334. Mencken, "George Ade," in *Prejudices: First Series* (New York: Knopf, 1919) 121.

paragraph length, which characterize these different forms. As Mencken wrote more frequently for books and magazines, this versatility would increase.

Mencken's artistic development differed from that of Mark Twain, Stephen Crane, Theodore Dreiser, and Ernest Hemingway, all of whom began as journalists but then turned to prose fiction. Journalism would remain Mencken's constant interest. While Mencken wrote proficiently enough to sell twenty-five short stories and even began a novel, he recognized by the age of twenty-four that his talents lay with prose nonfiction in its various forms.[20] This early recognition greatly facilitated Mencken's growth. At a young age he achieved something that has eluded many an older author: objectivity about one's own work.

In 1903, Mencken subscribed to a clipping service and pasted in sturdy scrapbooks all of the comments about his work. Mencken did not do this out of vanity, which was never one of his faults. His Germanic sense of order probably accounted in part for this: responsible people keep their records straight. But there was more. Mencken suspected, it seems, that his career would prove important, and the next period in his life—when he defended Dreiser and published Fitzgerald, battled the president and acquired a national reputation—would confirm his premonition.

---

[20]Mencken, "HLM, 1937," EPFL. Quoted by Adler, *The Mencken Bibliography*, 127. See Douglas C. Stenerson, "Short-Story Writing: A Neglected Phase of Mencken's Literary Apprenticeship" *Menckeniana* 30 (Summer 1969): 8–13; and Vincent Fitzpatrick, "H. L. Mencken (12 September 1880–29 January 1956)" in *Dictionary of Literary Biography*, volume 147 of *American Magazine Journalists, 1900–1960*, second series (Detroit: Gale Research, 1994) 185.

CHAPTER 3

The Growth of a National Reputation: 1908-1919

The uplifters have sworn to put down the villainous practice of copulation in this fair republic, and I begin to suspect that they will do it.... Their ideal is a nation devoted to masturbation and the praise of God. The American of the future will do his lovemaking in the bathroom, and he will be found in the same place when his country is invaded.

–*Mencken to Theodore Dreiser, [after 14 January 1915], in* Dreiser-Mencken Letters: The Correspondence of Theodore Dresier & H. L. Mencken, 1907–1945

"All in all," Mencken wrote to Theodore Dreiser in 1909, "I find that I have too many irons in the fire. To get more time for the work that I want to do, I must withdraw some of them. I am getting along toward thirty, and it is time for me to be planning for the future."[1] Despite Mencken's vow to retrench, this period from late 1908 through 1919 proved far more diverse and productive than his apprenticeship. In 1899, the obscure cigar salesman had

---

[1] Mencken to Theodore Dreiser, 7 March 1909, in *Dreiser-Mencken Letters: The Correspondence of Theodore Dreiser and H. L. Mencken, 1907–1945*, 2 volumes, ed. Thomas P. Riggio (Philadelphia: University of Pennsylvania Press) 22.

hustled a newspaper job through sheer perseverance. During his thirties, Mencken attained the enviable but demanding position of having too much to write. As Mencken's skill and confidence increased, he ranged more easily from scholarship to burlesque. The scholarly Mencken arranged for the translations of two plays by Henrik Ibsen and wrote the introductions and notes to them. Mencken wrote several essays on aesthetics, produced the first edition of *The American Language*, and engaged in a lively epistolary with the wealthy socialist Robert Rives La Monte. A mixture of seriousness and frivolity marked *A Little Book in C Major*, the collection of epigrams published in 1916. Influenced here by Mark Twain, Ambrose Bierce, Oscar Wilde, and Friedrich Nietzsche, Mencken lampooned the sacred cows and made his readers chuckle, perhaps despite themselves. Mencken the skeptic defined theology as the "effort to explain the unknowable by putting it in terms of the not worth knowing." "It is a sin to believe evil of others," jibed the classicist who laughed at the notion of humankind's perfectibility, "but it is seldom a mistake."[2] In *Heliogabalus*, a play upon which he and George Jean Nathan began to collaborate in 1919, he engaged in pure buffoonery: one of the scenes featured a bed holding nineteen people.

For the *Sunpapers*, Mencken stirred up his fellow Baltimoreans more than he ever had before. Moreover, he acquired his first regular column for a newspaper outside the city. Heretofore, Mencken had averaged four or five contributions a year to magazines. Now, he acquired a monthly book-review column for the *Smart Set*, the magazine that he and Nathan later came to edit with considerable skill. Mencken's books increased in number and, for the most part, in quality. Between 1917 and 1919, he published four volumes of consequence. Through these different forums—newspaper columns that appeared at various intervals, the magazine that appeared each month, and the books

---

[2] Mencken, *A Little Book in C Major* (New York: Lane, 1916) 75, 53.

that were published with greater frequency—Mencken saw his reputation grow locally and nationally.

After the Baltimore *Evening Sun* was founded in 1910, Mencken was appointed editor without title and wrote two or three pieces each day for the editorial page. From May 1911 until the fall of 1915, he reveled in the high jinks of "The Free Lance." Highly informal, the product of a seemingly tireless writer with a fecund and ironic imagination, this daily column offered an amalgam of aphorisms, lively hortatory passages, absurd quotations gleaned from a variety of sources, reproductions of garish advertisements, and jokes about the follies of local politicians. More than once, the heated Mencken ran out of space, and the column stopped abruptly *in medias res*, to be continued the next day.

Mencken wrote, as he explained it, "to combat, chiefly by ridicule, American piety, stupidity, tin-pot moralism, cheap chauvinism in all their forms."[3] In the column's early days, he was forbidden to criticize any church or members of the clergy, but when the clergy attacked Mencken, this restriction was lifted. Afterward, he jabbed his lance as he pleased: at incompetent cooks and Christian scientists, at osteopaths and anti-vivisectionists, at the moralists whom he scornfully dubbed "smut-hounds" and "virtuosi of virtue."[4] Baltimore had never seen such a column before, and never would again.

In the midst of so much controversy, Mencken showed a sense of fair play, even generosity, to his opponents. One of the clergymen who had expressed indignation about Mencken's writing was arrested with a naked Boy Scout at the local YMCA. Rather than gloat, Mencken wrote nothing at the time, secured the

---

[3]Ernest Boyd, *H. L. Mencken* (New York: McBride, 1925) 40–41.
[4]Mencken, "Autobiographical Notes, 1925," EPFL. Quoted by Betty Adler, *H. L. M.: The Mencken Bibliography* (Baltimore: Enoch Pratt Free Library, 1961) 49. Mencken, "The Free Lance," Baltimore *Evening Sun*, 8 July 1911.

clergyman's release, and hurried him out of town.[5] In addition, Mencken controlled the editorial mail and made certain to publish the most violent denunciations of him and his writing. In the end, "The Free Lance" greatly benefitted both Mencken and Baltimore journalism. The many attacks forced Mencken to emerge from this column better skilled in literary combat. Moreover, "The Free Lance" accustomed Baltimoreans to what Mencken called "the freest imaginable of free discussion," a right that the *Sunpapers* has tried to guard over the decades, a right that Mencken valued above all others.[6]

From June 1917 until July of the following year, Mencken wrote two or three columns per week, about 120 pieces in all, for the New York *Evening Mail*, his first protracted exposure to a newspaper audience outside Baltimore. Mencken thought highly enough of these columns—more formal and of considerably greater literary value than the writing in "The Free Lance"—to reprint several of them in subsequent anthologies.[7] As usual, Mencken's journalism touched upon a variety of subjects: literature (columns about Dreiser, George Ade, and Mark Twain), philology, music, penology, education (columns colorfully entitled "Under the Campus Pump"), men and women, food, and fashion. The two columns that attracted the most attention then, and remain most notorious today, discussed the history of the bathtub and the American South as a cultural wasteland.

---

[5] William Manchester, *Disturber of the Peace: The Life of H. L. Mencken* (New York: Harper, 1950) 62. Mencken mentions this matter in *Newspaper Days* (New York: Knopf, 1941) 28, but does not mention "The Free Lance."

[6]Mencken, "Autobiographical Notes, 1925," EPFL, 25. Quoted by Adler, *The Mencken Bibliography*, 49. For further discussion of "The Free Lance," see W. H. A. Williams, *H. L. Mencken* (Boston: Hall, 1977) 49–57; James W. Shutt, "H. L. Mencken and the Baltimore *Evening Sun* Free Lance Column," *Menckeniana* 48 (Winter 1973): 8–10; and Thomas G. Welshko, "The Free Lance" (1 and 2) *Menckeniana* 69 (Spring 1979): 9–12 and 70 (Summer 1979): 11–14.

[7]Manchester, *Disturber of the Peace*, 105.

In late 1917, the *Evening Mail* ran "A Neglected Anniversary," better known as Mencken's "bathtub hoax." Facetiously, he chronicles "one of the most important profane anniversaries in American history, to wit, the seventy-fifth anniversary of the introduction of the bathtub into These States." According to Mencken, the Cincinnati merchant Adam Thompson deserved credit for this momentous event, and President Millard Fillmore (fill the tub more) installed the first bathtub in the White House in early in 1851.[8] The reception of this "tissue of absurdities" reinforced Mencken's belief in the credulity of the American public, those gullible creatures who, as he laughingly recounted elsewhere, supported such ventures as the "Physicians Institute of Chicago, a foundation devoted to the development of the human bust by correspondence."[9] Despite Mencken's published statements that he had written a hoax, his "history" of the bathtub made its way into books; to this day, various media report this fabrication as fact.

In November 1917, the month prior to the appearance of the bathtub hoax, Mencken had published "The Sahara of the Bozart." Both columns showed Mencken's penchant for the absurd. With "Bozart," the man who loved neologisms offered the preposterous American rendering of the French phrase *beaux arts*. But Mencken's "Sahara," unlike "A Neglected Anniversary," discussed a serious issue, the demise of a culture that had once flourished:

---

[8]Mencken, "A Neglected Anniversary," New York *Evening Mail*, 28 December 1917. Included in *A Mencken Chrestomathy* (New York: Knopf, 1949) 592–97; and in *The Impossible H. L. Mencken: A Collection of His Best Newspaper Stories,* ed. Marion Elizabeth Rodgers (New York: Doubleday, 1991) 612–616.

[9]Mencken, "Melancholy Reflections," *Chicago Sunday Tribune*, 23 May 1926. Quoted at greater length by Adler, *The Mencken Bibliography*, 56. Mencken, "The Free Lance," Baltimore *Evening Sun*, 22 May 1913.

I leave it to any fair observer to find anything approaching culture in the South today. It is as if the Civil War stamped out all the bearers of the torch and left only a mob of peasants on the field. In all that gargantuan empire there is not a single orchestra capable of playing a Beethoven symphony, nor a single opera house, nor a single monument or building (less than fifteen years old) worth looking at.... Once your have counted James Branch Cabell you will not find a single Southern novelist whose work shows any originality or vitality.

Mencken could hardly have offered a more sweeping indictment of the fine arts in the American South.[10]

Although some Southerners might have dismissed it as such, this was not the diatribe of a Yankee who hated the South. No Quentin Compson wrestling with his heritage, Mencken appreciated Baltimore's Southern flavor, the ambiance that helped to make his life there so comfortable. In fact, with the conservative's pastoral vision, Mencken looked back fondly upon the antebellum South, "which produced a civilization of manifold excellences, and lavish fruits." With his penchant for hyperbole, Mencken was using the *Evening Mail* to prod Southern artists into restoring their region to its rightful cultural prominence. Mencken expanded this column considerably and included it in *Prejudices: Second Series*, where it generated a far greater response than it had in the newspaper. As Fred Hobson has shown so well in *Serpent in Eden: H. L. Mencken and the South*, Mencken's "Sahara" helped to effect the Southern Literary Renaissance of the 1920s.[11]

---

[10]Mencken, "The Sahara of the Bozart," New York *Evening Mail,"* 13 November 1917. An expanded version is included in *A Mencken Chrestomathy*, 184–95; the column is also included in *The Impossible H. L. Mencken*, ed. Marion Elizabeth Rodgers 491–94.

[11]Mencken, "The Sahara of the Bozart," in *Prejudices: Second Series* (New York: Knopf, 1920) 136–54. Fred Hobson, *Serpent in Eden: H. L. Mencken* (Chapel Hill: University of North Carolina Press, 1974).

While Mencken used his "Sahara" to challenge Southern culture, he was challenged himself, as both an editor and a book reviewer, to improve all of American literature through his association with the *Smart Set*. Mencken helped to edit this New York City monthly for more than nine years; over the span of more than fifteen, he wrote 182 book-review essays. When Mencken began with the *Smart Set* in November 1908, he found a national literature hampered by "complacency and conformity," a literature where "no novel that told the truth about life as Americans were living it...had a chance."[12]

Mencken sensed that American culture had never cast aside the pernicious influence of Puritanism, which he defined sardonically as "the haunting fear that someone, somewhere, may be happy."[13] This national culture, as Mencken viewed it, had never attained intellectual freedom and, unlike its European counterpart, judged literature not by its artistic merit but rather by its moral orthodoxy. Mencken encountered a culture in which Walt Whitman's *Leaves of Grass*, a landmark in American poetry, could be considered a dirty book, a culture that permitted *Huckleberry Finn*, in Mencken's view the best American novel ever written, to be banned from a public library. Mencken confronted a mentality that refused to accept Dreiser's *Sister Carrie*, the novel that, as much as any other one, made possible modern American literature. Like Shaw and Nietzsche, Dreiser challenged moral convention. He created a protagonist who, instead of being punished for her sexual activity, receives financial reward. Dreiser suggested that, in the impersonal, highly commercial society of late-nineteenth-century America, Carrie Meeber's most salable commodity is herself. After *Sister Carrie* was published in 1900, Dreiser earned $68.40, and the novel's reception drove him to the verge of suicide. As an editor and critic, Mencken battled against a culture that stifled the development of

---

[12]Mencken, "Fifteen Years," *Smart Set* 72 (December 1923): 139–40.
[13]Mencken, *A Mencken Chrestomathy*, 624.

an indigenous American literature that could speak freely. Part of Mencken's efforts entailed the publication and discussion of foreign authors—in part, certainly, because of the excellence of such writing but also in the hope of contrasting its more cosmopolitan perspective to the moral mania plaguing American letters.

More than any other periodical, the *Smart Set* served as the most significant national forum for Mencken's interest in American fiction. This coupling of man and magazine, which helped both parties as well as American literature, marked one of the most striking incongruities in Mencken's career. Founded in 1900 by William D'Alton Mann, a colorful Civil War veteran and railroad man, the *Smart Set* was designed to function as the literary counterpart of *Town Topics*, Mann's gossip magazine. The *Smart Set* contained 160 pages, plus 20 pages of advertising. Each issue began with a novelette, continued with several short stories (one in French), included an essay and poems, and offered a variety of shorter forms intended for comedy—aphorisms and dialogues, for example—that sometimes succeeded in being funny. Mann subtitled the *Smart Set* "A Magazine of Cleverness" and offered it as entertainment for an ostensibly refined readership.[14] The ribald Baltimorean, who borrowed a marble slab from a cemetery for use as a free-lunch counter, hardly seemed suited for a magazine that tried so hard to be chic, a periodical whose cover sported a masked Mephisto dangling hearts before Cupid's bow.

In October 1909, eleven months after Mencken's first book review appeared, Nathan began his column on the theater. In 1911, Mann sold the *Smart Set* to John Adams Thayer, and in early 1913

---

[14]Carl Richard Dolmetsch, *The Smart Set: A History and Anthology* (New York: Dial, 1966) 9–10, 5, 6. Professor Dolmetsch's book offers a far more detailed treatment than I can provide here, and I would direct the interested reader to this valuable study. Frank Luther Mott's chapter on the *Smart Set* in *A History of American Magazines* (Volume 5): *Sketches of 21 Magazines, 1905–1930* (Cambridge MA.: Harvard University Press, 1968) is, like the rest of his monumental study, thorough and informative.

Thayer appointed Willard Huntington Wright as editor. Better
known to posterity as S. S. Van Dine, the pseudonym under which
he later wrote the highly popular Philo Vance detective stories,
Wright bravely published Max Beerbohm and D. H. Lawrence.
But with advertising and circulation declining, Thayer feared that
the magazine was growing too bold and fired Wright at the end of
the year. Mencken snorted that the *Smart Set*, after Wright's
dismissal, was "as righteous as a decrepit and converted
madame."[15] In August 1914, hurt by the panic on Wall Street that
followed the beginning of World War I, Thayer unloaded the
magazine, and Eltinge F. Warner, who had succeeded with *Field
& Stream*, became publisher of the *Smart Set* as well.[16] Warner
asked Nathan to edit the magazine, and Nathan agreed on the
condition that he and Mencken work together. The issue of
October 1914, their first, carried a strident motto on its cover:
"One civilized reader is worth a thousand boneheads."[17]

Before they could attract more civilized readers, Mencken
and Nathan first had to deal with two major problems: the *Smart
Set*'s position regarding World War I and the magazine's unstable
finances. Although the magazine was bombarded by "at least 50
war poems a day from the hog and hominy belts," the editors
ignored the war, a wise decision given Mencken's sympathies.[18]
Mencken and Nathan responded with equal sense to the
magazine's debt. Among other measures, they engaged cheaper
offices, sometimes drew no salaries, and wrote a sizable amount of
copy under a variety of pseudonyms. Moreover, they founded pulp
magazines—the *Parisienne* in 1915 and *Saucy Stories* the
following year—to keep the *Smart Set* afloat. Finally, they

---

[15]Mencken to Theodore Dreiser, 18 March [1914], in Riggio, *Dreiser-
Mencken Letters*, 134.

[16]Dolmetsch, *The Smart Set*, 44

[17]Carl Richard Dolmetsch, "Mencken as Magazine Editor," *Menckeniana*
21 (Spring 1967): 3.

[18] Mencken to Louis Untermeyer, 3 November [1916], in *The Letters of H.
L. Mencken*, ed. Guy J. Forgue (New York: Knopf, 1961) 94.

continued the low rate of pay, one cent per word for prose contributions and twenty-five cents per line for poetry, instituted by Mann. The joke circulated that "writing for the *Smart Set*...is more fun than being paid for it."[19] But writers kept submitting manuscripts, sometimes more than six hundred each month.[20] Mencken and Nathan devised an efficient and humane way for handling submissions. Mencken read all manuscripts first, and his veto killed a submission. If Mencken liked the manuscript, then he sent it along to Nathan, whose approval was also necessary for acceptance. All manuscripts, then, were read by at least one editor, and authors received a quick response to their writing. Frequently, encouragement, incisive criticism, and suggestions as to where else the manuscript might be submitted accompanied letters of rejection. Moreover, the *Smart Set* paid upon acceptance rather than upon publication. The editors' courtesy, competence, and charisma generally overcame the magazine's penury.

Under the Mencken-Nathan editorship foreign authors retained a forum for their writing. Aldous Huxley appeared in the *Smart Set*, as did Somerset Maugham, with his controversial story "Miss Thompson" (the basis for the highly successful play *Rain*). Moreover, the *Smart Set* was the first American periodical to publish James Joyce, with the Irishman contributing "The Boarding House" and "A Little Cloud," two stories from *Dubliners*.

Although Mencken complained that he and Nathan were perpetually hamstrung by the censors, the *Smart Set* managed to publish writing of at least equal quality by American authors, fledgling and established.[21] Theodore Dreiser appeared here, as

---

[19]Dolmetsch, "Mencken as Magazine Editor," 6.

[20]Carl Richard Dolmetsch, "'HLM' and 'GJN': The Editorial Partnership Re-examined," *Menckeniana* 75 (Fall 1980): 30.

[21]Mencken, *A Book of Prefaces* (New York: Knopf, 1917) 277.

did Sherwood Anderson, Willa Cather, and F. Scott Fitzgerald.[22] Carl Dolmetsch, author of the magazine's definitive history, has called the *Smart Set* "a magazine of neglected, though inestimable, value to literary history as the proving grounds, between 1900 and 1924, of more literary careers...than any other journal every published in America."[23] Hardly the sole contributors to such success—they edited the *Smart Set* for less than half of this period—Mencken and Nathan still figured prominently in the magazine's distinguished literary history.

While Mencken's achievements as an editor benefitted American letters, he wielded even more influence as a critic. Mencken had written criticism previously and would continue to discuss literature after he left the *Smart Set*, but it was during his first ten or eleven years of this association that his reputation as a literary critic reached its zenith. Everyone, it seems, wanted Mencken's opinion, and during some years he received a staggering one thousand books to review. He read quickly, usually lying down and rarely bothering to take notes or to mark up the book. In the monthly essays that ran to several thousand words, lengthy discussions of the books that he considered most important and capsule commentaries upon others, Mencken ranged across the continents and among the genres. He discussed the plays of Ibsen and George Moore, the philosophy of Nietzsche and Henry Bergson, and the novels of H. G. Wells and Arnold Bennett. Among American authors, Mencken reviewed the criticism of Van Wyck Brooks and the prose fiction of Sherwood Anderson, Theodore Dreiser, Willa Cather, Hamlin Garland, and F. Scott Fitzgerald—the list ran into the hundreds. In the midst of so many other duties, Mencken ignored relatively little of consequence during these years.

---

[22]See Bode, *Mencken* (Carbondale IL: Southern Illinois University Press, 1977) 74–75 for a more detailed listing.

[23]Dolmetsch, *The Smart Set*, 44.

Despite such productivity and the acclaim of many, Mencken never considered himself primarily a literary critic. He recognized during his lifetime, as a number of critics have perceived subsequently, the remarkable consistency of his thought: his writing was of one piece, no matter what particular subject he happened to be discussing. The traits that most affected Mencken's response to the American scene at large—his nationalism, autodidacticism, iconoclasm, fatalism, and rationalism—shaped his response to literature. In these *Smart Set* reviews and in his other pieces on literature, Mencken discussed some writers with considerable acuity: Joseph Conrad, for example, whom Mencken praised before it became fashionable to do so; and Edgar Allan Poe, whose importance, Mencken recognized early, lay as a critic rather than as a poet or an author of short stories. On the other hand, some of Mencken's judgments give one pause, and one comes to question a perspective that, at times, seems parochial. Mencken was, in brief, a literary critic with obvious strengths and weaknesses.[24]

Despite his early books on Shaw and Nietzsche and his success in publishing prominent foreign authors in the *Smart Set*, Mencken finally proved most interested in, and knowledgeable about, American literature. In Mencken's literary criticism, one hears echoes of his political commentary before both World Wars: do not be duped by the British; resist England's efforts to use America for its own purposes. Mencken the Anglophobe stressed the need for American autonomy and praised originality rather than imitation. He repeatedly called for an indigenous American literature rather than, as he remarked graphically, "an out-house of English literature."[25] As Mencken glanced back over American fiction, he anticipated Ernest Hemingway's famous remark in

---

[24]The following discussion of Mencken's literary criticism is hardly comprehensive. See William Nolte's valuable study, *H. L. Mencken: Literary Critic* (Middletown, CT.: Wesleyan University Press, 1966).

[25]Mencken, "Mainly Fiction," *Smart Set* 58 (March 1919): 139. See Nolte, *H. L. Mencken: Literary Critic*, 231.

Green Hills of Africa by speaking of Mark Twain as "the true father of our national literature, the first genuinely American artist of the royal blood."[26] Mencken saw in Dreiser's novels not only their American setting but also their peculiarly American sensibility; no foreign author, Mencken recognized, could have told the story of Frank Cowperwood, the protagonist of Dreiser's *Trilogy of Desire*. On the other hand, Mencken called Henry James "no more an American than the Sultan of Sulu."[27] Like Mark Twain's Jim wondering why a Frenchman can't talk like a man, Mencken wondered why James, born in New York City, could not write in an American English that could actually be understood.

Mencken the autodidact wrote just as unkindly of the efforts of the American academy. The man who later ridiculed Franklin Roosevelt's Brain Trust lampooned the professors laboring "in one-building universities on the prairie, still hoping, at the age of sixty, to get their whimsical essays into the *Atlantic Monthly*."[28] Mencken went so far as to label the majority of the average college faculty "a rabble of quacks and racketeers." After asking why colleges retained such frauds, the man who always thought "mass education" an oxymoron proceeded to answer his own question: "Superior men would be wasted on the job of educating the uneducable, and maybe be driven insane. The best professor for an idiot is a quack—and that is what American colleges provide for him, whether deliberately or by natural law. The two understand and esteem each other. What the one can't teach is precisely what the other doesn't want to learn. They are happy together in a perfect symbiosis."[29] Mencken, as William Nolte has

---

[26]Mencken, "The Burden of Humor," *Smart Set* 39 (February 1913): 152.

[27]Mencken, "The Leading American Novelist," *Smart Set* 33 (January 1911): 163.

[28]Mencken, "Suite Americaine," in *Prejudices: Third Series* (New York: Knopf, 1922) 320.

[29]Mencken, "Four Glad Years," *College Humor* 66 (March 1934): 9.

remarked, "was hated and feared more than any other American of his day by the average university teacher."[30] It is easy to see why. Attacking what he viewed as the professors' ignorance, timidity, pretense, and lack of intellectual curiosity, Mencken denigrated the academic critics early in the century, the New Humanists during the 1920s, and the New Critics later. Mencken saw the jobs of professor and critic as mutually exclusive: the "true professor" is "especially fit for aesthetic autopsies," while the "true critic" is "fit for aesthetic obstetrics."[31] Mencken could hardly have chosen a more patronizing, or more reductive, metaphor. In this remarkably simple scheme of things, he saw himself, of course, as an agent of light rather than darkness, as an obstetrician rather than a literary coroner. Mencken's task, as he presented it, was to resist the academic mentality that "worked steadily, maliciously, and lamentably against the recognition of every new writer who has anything sound and original to contribute to the national letters, from Poe to Whitman, from Whitman to Mark Twain to Dreiser."[32] Like Edmund Wilson, who later battled with the Modern Language Association over its editions of the American classics, Mencken believed that the national literature suffered at the hands of those ostensibly supporting it.

Whereas Mencken's autodidacticism generated his battle with the professors, his iconoclasm effected his attack upon the literary establishment, the literature of what George Santayana called the "Genteel Tradition."[33] Such writing, in Mencken's view, lacked the courage to deal with an American experience characterized by revolt rather than by acquiescence. Mencken labored to sweep aside what he scornfully dubbed "the ashes of New England," to

---

[30]Nolte, *H. L. Mencken: Literary Critic*, 125.

[31]Mencken, "The National Letters," *Smart Set* 54 (February 1918): 138.

[32]Mencken, "Critics Wild and Tame," *Smart Set* 53 (December 1917): 139.

[33]See George H. Douglas, *H. L. Mencken: Critic of American Life* (Hamden, CT: Archon Books, 1974) 184–85.

overturn what he saw as nothing more than "a bowl of mush."[34] Although Mencken chastised a number of writers for their timidity, he attacked William Dean Howells and Henry James most frequently and ferociously.

Prior to his death in 1920, Howells had acquired, through both his criticism and his novels, a considerable reputation as the "Dean of American Letters." In Mencken's view, however, Howells had proven a negative influence upon Mark Twain. Howells's sensibility was so genteel, Mencken remarked contemptuously, that the novelist had composed only "a long row of hollow and uninspired books, with no more ideas in them than so many empty volumes of the *Ladies' Home Journal*."[35] When Mencken began to write for the *Smart Set*, Henry James had already produced *The Wings of the Dove*, *The Ambassadors*, and *The Golden Bowl*, the major achievements of his renowned "later" period. But the Mencken who insisted upon clarity found odious the complexities of the Jamesian style. Moreover, Mencken believed that James's sheltered perspective precluded a full understanding of the harsher realities of the American scene. James, Mencken snorted famously, "would have vastly improved by a few whiffs from the [Chicago stockyards.]"[36]

Mencken treated both authors unfairly. The remark about James and the stockyards is facile invective, not judicious criticism, and Mencken showed no appreciation of the psychological complexity distinguishing James's writing. Moreover, Howells was hardly the timid figure whom he caricatured. Among all the major American writers, Howells alone

---

[34]Mencken, "The National Letters," in *Prejudices: Second Series* (New York: Knopf, 1920) 18. Mencken, "The American Novel," Baltimore *Evening Sun*, 27 August 1923.

[35]Mencken, "Gropings in Literary Darkness," *Smart Set* 63 (October 1920): 139–40. Mencken, "Variations in G Minor," Baltimore *Evening Sun*, 11 May 1916. Mencken, "The Dean," in *Prejudices: First Series* (New York: Knopf, 1919) 53.

[36]Mencken, "Notes in the Margin," *Smart Set* 63 (November 1920): 141.

publicly defended those arrested at the Haymarket Riot in Chicago in 1886. In addition, had Mencken bothered to juxtapose *The Rise of Silas Lapham* (1885) with *A Hazard of New Fortunes* (1890), he would have perceived the more forceful irony and more candid realism of the later novel. However, the inaccuracy of Mencken's censure finally proves less significant than his decision to assault such figures. Early in his career, Mencken learned that one can neither establish nor maintain a reputation by drubbing inconsequential opponents. The iconoclast who heaved dead cats at American presidents and Baltimore's guardians of public virtue found nothing sacrosanct about prominent literary figures.

For Mencken the fatalist, God was not in his heaven, and all was far from right with the world. Mencken saw idealism as humankind's curse, and he criticized America as a place "where hope is a sort of national vice."[37] A determinist rather than a believer in free will, Mencken saw humankind as the prisoner of heredity and environment, with the former a stronger, more destructive force. Mencken's fatalism drew him to the gloomy Naturalism of Emile Zola in France, Thomas Hardy in England, and Theodore Dreiser in America. Their fictional universes, where the forlorn miners in Zola's *Germinal*, Hardy's Tess Durbeyfield and Michael Henchard, and Dreiser's Jennie Gerhardt act so ineffectually in the face of forces confronting them, corresponded to Mencken's view of the human predicament. It was a bold lie, Mencken always believed, that someone has to win in the game of life.

Mencken's fatalism also showed itself in his propensity for black humor, the laughter of the damned. To understand Mencken's perspective here, one must look beneath the facade of his laughter; much of the time, it was hardly lighthearted. Had Mencken lived later into the century, he might well have admired the macabre humor marking such novels as Joseph Heller's *Catch-*

---

[37]Mencken, "The Forward Looker," in *Prejudices: Third Series* (New York: Knopf, 1922) 226.

22 and John Irving's *The World According to Garp.* Mencken appreciated Ambrose Bierce's *The Devil's Dictionary* and Mark Twain's *The Mysterious Stranger*, whose underlying vision resembled the perspective that generated so much rueful laughter on Mencken's part. Rejecting the stereotype of Mark Twain as a "light-hearted and kindly old clown," Mencken stressed the pervasive, sardonic irony distinguishing his favorite novelist's later books. And Bierce, Mencken remarked appreciatively, "put man, intellectually, somewhere between the sheep and the horned cattle, and as a hero somewhere below the rats.... Out of the spectacle of life about him he got an unflagging and Gargantuan joy."[38] So did Mencken, who was detailing his own position as much as Bierce's.

As a literary critic, the Mencken who spoke of the "eternal tragedy of man" had only contempt for uplifting literature, a hoax perpetrated by the unenlightened upon the credulous. Mencken lambasted "the typically American, the optimistic, the inspirational, the *Saturday Evening Post* school" of literature.[39] This same attitude made Mencken cast a cold eye upon all reformers and their schemes. Here as elsewhere, Mencken's comments about American literature mirrored his comments on American life.

Not surprisingly, this man who spoke with such certitude, who so loved the majestic euphony of the universal statement, who so relished hyperbole, could be laughably wrong about literature. Mencken declared boldly that "Mark Twain...produced at least four books that were better than 'The Scarlet Letter.'"[40] This judgment is unconscionable, unless Mencken had the good fortune to discover somewhere three books that the rest of us have never seen. As a critic of poetry, Mencken made some bizarre

---

[38]Mencken, "The Man Within," in *A Mencken Chrestomathy* (New York: Knopf, 1949) 486. Mencken, "Ambrose Bierce," in *A Mencken Chrestomathy*, 493–94.

[39]Mencken, *Happy Days* (New York: Knopf, 1940) 98. Mencken "Repetition Generale," *Smart Set* 61 (January 1920): 53.

[40]Mencken, "The Free Lance," Baltimore *Evening Sun*, 20 November 1912.

declarations. He called poetry "a violent and irreconcilable enemy to the intellect.... What it essays to do, in brief, is to make life more bearable in an intolerable world by obliterating and concealing all the harsher realities. Its message is that all will be well by next Tuesday."[41] Mencken made this remark in 1924, two years after T. S. Eliot's *The Waste Land* was published. Moreover, Mencken sometimes showed a lack of objectivity that hindered him in different ways. On the one hand, he was incapable of a nonpartisan undertaking such as Edmund Wilson's *Axel's Castle*. This account of literary Modernism is an astute analysis of writers about whom the author had marked reservations. On the other hand, Mencken sometimes allowed his enthusiasm to conquer his critical judgment. More than once, especially during his early years, Mencken served as cheerleader and press agent rather than as a supposedly disinterested evaluator.

Just as important, Mencken's thoroughgoing rationalism severely limited his ability to deal with modern literature. This "materialist of materialists," as he called himself, declared that "'literature dealing with facts' is my province in criticism.... I am predominantly a reviewer of ideas and the more squarely those ideas are based upon demonstrable facts the better I like them."[42] Clearly, Mencken's critical system was best suited for mimetic fiction, those works of art that, as much as possible, hold the mirror up to nature. Given this bias, Realism and Naturalism, those schools demonstrating what he called "representational fidelity," interested Mencken more than Romanticism.[43] With James Branch Cabell being the most notable exception, Mencken did not like authors who engaged in flights of fantasy.

---

[41]Mencken, "Poetry in American." *Chicago Sunday Tribune*, 30 November 1924.

[42]Mencken to Henry Sydnor Harrison, 24 November 1916, in Forgue, *Letters*, 98. Mencken to Ivan J. Kramoris, 8 January 1940, in *The New Mencken Letters*, ed. Carl Bode (New York: Dial Press, 1977) 455.

[43]Mencken, "The Novel," in *Prejudices: Third Series*, 205

Modernism, as a number of critics have remarked, is Neo-Romanticism. Mencken was either unwilling or unable to deal with many of the complexities that marked the novel as the twentieth century progressed: extensive understatement, a literature of silence speaking more through what is left out than through what is included; a fictional framework of myth and allusion; stream of consciousness and interior monologue; the use of the relativist perspective rather than the conventional first- or third-person narrator; the absence of a conventional plot; and the movement of a text according to psychological time rather than straightforward chronology. Discussing the experimental technique of Gertrude Stein, for example, Mencken embarrassed himself by remarking that "it is the great achievement of Miss Stein that she has made English easier to write and harder to read."[44] Moreover, he failed to come to terms with Joyce's *Ulysses* as well as Faulkner's novels.

In all, however, Mencken's strengths as a critic outnumbered his deficiencies. When Mencken began his *Smart Set* reviews in his late twenties, he had not yet fully articulated his aesthetic system. His methodology, therefore, developed as his abilities did. Mencken sensibly constructed a system that employed his considerable skills as a stylist and as an impressionistic critic bringing extensive ancillary knowledge to the text under scrutiny.

"Write what you damn well please," Mencken was instructed when he joined the *Smart Set*, "as long as it's lively and gets attention."[45] For Mencken, true critics had to be artists themselves, figures striving to "make an articulate noise in the world."[46] Offering both evaluation and entertainment, this critic as catalyst was obligated "to provoke the reaction between the work of art and the spectator."[47] To Mencken's credit, one rarely finishes one

[44]Mencken, "A Review of Reviews," *Smart Set* 4 (October 1914): 158–59.

[45]Dolmetsch, *The Smart Set*, 24.

[46]Mencken, "Footnote on Criticism," in *Prejudices: Third Series*, 84–85.

[47]Mencken, "Criticism of Criticism of Criticism," in *Prejudices: First Series* (New York: Knopf, 1919) 20.

of his reviews feeling bored. Consider, for example, Mencken's discussions of Dreiser's books. As an editor and literary agent, pitchman and public defender, Mencken did appreciably more for Dreiser than any other individual ever did. However, Dreiser's deficiencies as a stylist irritated Mencken, as did what Mencken viewed as Dreiser's propensity for squandering his talent on ventures for which he was not temperamentally suited. Some of Dreiser's worst writing generated some of Mencken's finest.

Mencken viewed *The "Genius,"* the patently autobiographical novel published in 1915, as Dreiser's least distinguished novel up that time. In a review waggishly entitled "A Literary Behemoth," Mencken did not merely criticize the book's prolixity; rather, he spoke of a "novel so huge that a whole shift of critics are needed to read it.... I read only the first and last paragraphs of each chapter. The rest I farmed out to my wife, to my cousin Ferd, to my pastor and my beer man." Mencken did not merely assert that the novel suffers from a lack of form; rather, with his flair for analogy, he called *The "Genius"* "as shapeless as a Philadelphia pie woman." Rather than say that Dreiser's prose is turgid, Mencken the beer drinker huffed that "a greater regard for fairness of phrase and epithet would be as the flow of Pilsner to the weary reader in his journey across the vast deserts, steppes and pampas of the Dreiserian fable."[48] Dreiser, understandably, did not applaud Mencken's performance.

Mencken's burlesque of *Hey Rub-A-Dub-Dub*, Dreiser's clumsy effort to write metaphysics, made the novelist just as unhappy. A more conventional writer might well have said in print what Mencken stressed in his correspondence: that Dreiser's talent lay as a writer of mimetic fiction. But the stylist who took risks that others avoided opted for a more inventive approach in the *Smart Set.* "In every line...there is evidence of the author's antecedent agony," Mencken snickered. "One pictures Dreiser sitting up all night...wrestling with the insoluble, trying his

---

[48]Mencken, "A Literary Behemoth," *Smart Set* 47 (December 1915): 153.

darndest to penetrate the unknowable." The skeptic then shifted from exposition to narration and lampooned not only *Hey Rub-A-Dub-Dub* but also other matters that he found equally absurd:

> One o'clock strikes, and the fire sputters. Ghosts stalk in the room...the spooks of all men who have died for ideas since the world began.... Two o'clock. What, then, is the truth about marriage? Is it...a grand sweet song, or is it, as the gals in the Village say, a hideous mockery and masquerade, invented by Capitalism to enslave the soul of woman—a hideous *Schweinerei*? Three o'clock. Was Marx right or wrong, a seer or mere nose puller?...
> Back to Pontius Pilate. *Quod est veritas?*...Think of the brains gone to wreck struggling with this problem.... Four o'clock.... A gray fog without. Across the street two detectives rob a drunken man. Up at Tarrytown John D. Rockefeller snores in his damp Baptist bed, dreaming gaudily that he is young again and mashed on a girl named Marie.... A poor working-girl, betrayed by Moe the boss's son, drowns herself in the aquarium. It is late, ah me.... What the deuce, then, is God.[49]

Hey Rub-A-Dub-Dub is now discussed only infrequently as one of Dreiser's lesser efforts. But Mencken's imaginative universe in this review—the farcical tableau populated by the self-assured radicals in Greenwich Village, the Baptist in his damp bed stoked by sweet Marie, and the womanizer named Moe—continues to regale. With its lack of equivocation and self-conscious preciosity, with its wealth of invention and gusto and laughter, such prose has tempted many to try to write "like Mencken." No one has succeeded; some have looked foolish in the attempt. When he attained his mature style, Mencken was able, as much as any other

---

[49]Mencken, "More Notes from a Diary," *Smart Set* 62 (May 1920): 138-39.

critic who has ever written in America, to make a review a work of art in itself, to offer information and entertainment concurrently. Mencken's facility with impressionistic reviews also enhanced his literary criticism. To borrow William Nolte's apt analogy, Mencken used the text as a springboard to leap to those matters that interested him most.[50] Mencken always insisted that, for the good critic, "what is before him is always infinitely less interesting than what is within him."[51] Using the text as a point of departure, Mencken constructed reviews that more closely resemble the essays in today's *New York Review of Books* than the analyses carried by the academic quarterlies. Such impressionism succeeds or fails depending upon the breadth of the reviewers' knowledge and their ability to perceive connections that might well elude others. Mencken read extensively in the natural sciences, history, biography, and medicine.[52] He believed that his ability to incorporate such knowledge contributed to his criticism's wide appeal as well as to the hostility that it generated among more conventional critics.

In the end, the value of Mencken's literary criticism lay just as much in what it accomplished as in the stylistic facility and range of interests distinguishing it. Mencken always argued that criticism should be neither constructive nor didactic, but he did much good himself, and he helped to teach both his contemporaries and subsequent critics what is more important: namely, the writer's need to function freely. "I am absolutely against all censorships," he explained. "It seems to me far better that indecencies should go unchallenged by law than that gangs of fanatics and perverts should police us. I believe that every form of censorship...falls inevitably into the hands of such fanatics and perverts."[53] Even though Mencken had lampooned *The "Genius,"*

[50]Nolte, *H. L. Mencken: Literary Critic*, 100.
[51]Mencken, "Footnote on Criticism" in *Prejudices: Third Series*, 88.
[52]Mencken, "Autobiographical Notes, 1925," 70–77, EPFL.
[53]Ibid., 170, EPFL.

he spent considerable time and money battling for Dreiser when the novel was suppressed in 1916 by John Sumner, the successor to Anthony Comstock as the chief guardian of America's morals. During the next decade, Mencken fought just as ardently for an undistinguished essay in the *American Mercury*, and he defended James Branch Cabell and James T. Farrell when the "smut-hounds" turned their attention upon these novelists. "Whenever *A* annoys or injures *B* on the grounds of saving or improving *X*," the Baltimorean explained succinctly, "*A* is a scoundrel." He labeled this proposition, one of his most representative and frequently quoted statements, "Mencken's Law."[54]

Analogy, as Mencken well knew from his own writing, says more with less, and the tropes that recur in discussions of Mencken's literary criticism detail his efforts to lead America out of its repressive past into the light of day. Early in the century, as Van Wyck Brooks has remarked, Mencken cleared the way for writers of "foreign" stock, and later, as Charles Scruggs has shown so well, Mencken did "more than any other critic in American letters" to help African-American authors. Dreiser thanked Mencken for his efforts to "blaze new trails—seek poor sprouts under the weeds—& chop down all the choking ones for miles around."[55] Much later, as he assessed their mutual efforts, Dreiser chose a more bellicose analogy to capture Mencken's onslaught: "You proceeded to fight for me. Night and day apparently. Swack! Smack! Crack! Until finally you succeeded in chasing a whole nation of literary flies to cover."[56] Had Mencken the pathfinder hacked away less doggedly, had the assaults of this combative

[54] Mencken, *Newspaper Days: 1899–1906* (New York: Knopf, 1941) 38.

[55] Van Wyck Brooks, *The Confident Years: 1885–1915* (New York: Dutton, 1952) 4. Charles Scruggs, *The Sage in Harlem: H. L. Mencken and the Black Writers of the 1920s* (Baltimore: Johns Hopkins University Press,1984) 7. Dreiser to Mencken, 23 September 1920, in Riggio, *Dreiser-Mencken Letters*, 396.

[56] Dreiser to Mencken, 27 March 1943, in Riggio, *Dreiser-Mencken Letters*, 690. See Riggio, "Dreiser and Mencken: In the Literary Trenches," *American Scholar* 54 (Spring 1985): 227–38.

critic proved more timorous, American literature in the twentieth century might well have followed a different course.

Mencken's efforts to "clear the way for writers of genuine talent and honest intentions" distinguished a number of his books as well as his association with the *Smart Set.*[57] In *A Book of Prefaces* (1917), his single volume devoted entirely to literary criticism, Mencken baited those whom he held responsible for the unhealthiness of American letters. Never before had he written a book so consistently strident, and his opponents responded in kind. *Prefaces* marked the first of four important books published at the end of this decade. As we have seen, such productivity was due in considerable part to Mencken's decreased responsibilities as a journalist. Although Mencken could not discuss the fighting in Europe, he could, and did, wage war on the home front of American literature.

"Joseph Conrad," the first of Mencken's four chapters, offers a brief biographical sketch, the author's publication history, and a summary of the critical responses—a format continued in the essays about Theodore Dreiser and James Huneker. Mencken speaks approvingly of the lack of moral purpose in Conrad's writing and praises the novelist's pessimism, his willingness to acknowledge the heart of darkness beating in all of us. Moreover, Mencken applauds Conrad's black humor, his depiction of "the tragic struggles of the soul of man under the gross stupidity and obscene joking of the gods."[58] Such a remark can only insult the American believer whom Mencken views as, at best, unreflective.

The briefest of Mencken's essays, "James Huneker" discusses the least-remembered individual among the three. This critic of the seven arts, born in Philadelphia in 1856, published prolifically as a newspaper columnist, essayist, novelist, and autobiographer. Huneker, Mencken explains, has gained "celebrity

---

[57]Mencken, "Autobiographical Notes, 1907," 172, EPFL.
[58]Mencken, "Joseph Conrad," in *A Book of Prefaces* (New York: Knopf, 1917) 63.

abroad as the only critic of music that America has ever produced." Striking out once more at the American Philistine and at the dullness of academic criticism, Mencken applauds Huneker's attack upon the "pretentious donkey who presumes to do battle for...a 'sound' ethic—the 'forward looking' man...the conservator of orthodoxy...the rattler of ancient phrases." Three years later, Huneker responded in kind by praising Mencken as the "Attila of American criticism."[59]

"Theodore Dreiser" offers what was at this time the most comprehensive account of Dreiser's life and work. Mencken speaks with greater objectivity than he had previously—in the glowing review of *Jennie Gerhardt* in 1911, for example. Mencken derides, among other things, Dreiser's credulity and the extraneous detail marring his books. Dreiser was not pleased, and the men quarreled. Dreiser did not object, however, to the two provocative analogies in the essay's first paragraph. Mencken bemoans the dearth of worthwhile American fiction: "Out of the desert of American fictioneering, so populous and yet so dreary, Dreiser stands up." And when Mencken asserts that "there is something downright heroic in the way the man has held his narrow and perilous ground," he depicts American literature, once again, as a battlefield where enlightenment and provincial ignorance clash. Later, in an uncharacteristic allusion to Alexander Pope, Mencken speaks belligerently of Dreiser's struggle with "the New Dunciad," those academic critics as literary coroners who denigrate contemporary literature.[60] The final chapter of *Prefaces* makes this remark to Pope's dunces seem remarkably temperate.

"Puritanism as a Literary Force" stands as one of Mencken's most skillful and significant essays. Ninety-two pages long, the piece is more a monograph than a preface, and the title itself is a

---

[59]Mencken, "James Huneker," in *A Book of Prefaces*, 169, 193. Huneker's description of Mencken is quoted by Bode, *Mencken*, 186.

[60]Mencken, "Theodore Dreiser," in *A Book of Prefaces*, 67, 134.

misnomer. Although Mencken does discuss Puritanism's influence upon American literature, he shows far more interest in its influence upon all of American life. "That deep-seated and uncorrupted Puritanism," Mencken declares unequivocally, "that conviction of the pervasiveness of sin, of the supreme importance of moral correctness, of the need of savage and inquisitorial laws, has been a dominating force in America since the very beginning." Mencken, as George Douglas has shown, uses *Puritanism* rhetorically as a convenient catch-all for the negative aspects of the American experience.[61] Mencken attributes to Puritanism such things as the ubiquitous vice crusades and the endless searches for brummagem utopias. Puritanism, Mencken complains, has made Americans timid—they fear drink, sex, and the free exchange of ideas, in short, any form of enjoyment—and it has compelled them to see all issues in moral terms. Americans value reticence more than honesty; they deny the unattractive and inflate the commonplace. Puritanism, like democracy, is founded upon the envy of the inferior man for his betters. Puritanism generated Philistinism, Mencken laments, and he bemoans America's lack of intellectual curiosity. The iconoclast goes so far as to call his native land the "culture of the intellectually disinherited."[62]

A German-American of unpopular views during World War I, Mencken used all four essays to shout "I accuse!" at the citizens of his native land. Surely, he anticipated what was coming. Although *Prefaces* was praised in France, Mencken remarked, in a rare example of understatement, that the book "was manhandled by the orthodox reviewers" in America. Stuart Pratt Sherman, then a professor at the University of Illinois who had previously vilified Dreiser, reacted even more furiously to Mencken's essays. In "Beautifying American Letters," Sherman called Mencken a "member of the Germania Mannerchor [German male chorus]"

---

[61] Mencken, "Puritanism as a Literary Force," in *A Book of Prefaces*, 226. Douglas, *H. L. Mencken: Critic of American Life*, 83.
[62] Mencken, "Puritanism as a Literary Force," 5.

who edits an un-American magazine. Sherman explained that Mencken "is not a German. He was born in Baltimore…. That fact should silence the silly people who have suggested that he and Dreiser are the secret agents of the Wilhelmstrasse." Later, Sherman changed his mind and tried to make amends, but Mencken politely declined. Such an individual, Mencken noted sagely, "was too useful as an enemy to be wasted as a friend."[63]

When *In Defense of Women* appeared in 1918, the controversy continued, but it related in no way to World War I or to jingoistic critics like Sherman. Here, Mencken analyzed the battle of the sexes, the metaphor unifying the book. Drawing heavily upon material that had appeared in the *Smart Set*, Mencken finished *In Defense* in six weeks. The book sold slowly in its first printing by Philip Goodman. Alfred A. Knopf then took over the volume, which Mencken revised in 1922. It reached its eleventh printing by 1928 and was translated into French, German, and Hungarian. Financially, *In Defense* was Mencken's most successful book up to this time.[64] Certainly, the volume's topicality enhanced its sale; the woman's suffrage movement was growing, and the Nineteenth Amendment passed in 1920. More important, though, Mencken had written a witty study of a timeless subject, the bumpy passage of men and women through this vale of sorrow, and *In Defense* continues to this day to delight some and outrage others.

---

[63]Mencken, "George Jean Nathan, in *Prejudices: First Series*, 210. Stuart Pratt Sherman, "Beautifying American Letters," *The Nation* 105 (29 November 1917): 593–94. Mencken's remark about not wasting Sherman as a friend is from material not included in *Minority Report: The Notebooks of H. L. Mencken* and was published in *Menckeniana* 33 (Spring 1970): 1–2. For further discussion of the Mencken-Sherman conflict, see Nolte, *H. L. Mencken: Literary Critic*, 151–59; and Robert Bloom, "Past Indefinite: The Sherman-Mencken Debate on the American Tradition," *Western Humanities Review* 15 (Winter 1961): 73–81.

[64]Mencken, "HLM, 1937," EPFL. Quoted by Adler, *The Mencken Bibliography*, 8. Mencken and George Jean Nathan, *The American Credo: A Contribution toward the Interpretation of the National Mind* (New York: Knopf, 1920) 66.

"Love is the delusion," Mencken asserted, "that one woman differs from another."[65] Such flippancy caused some to view him, wrongly, as a misogynist. Had Mencken encountered the aphorism reversed—that is, "Love is the delusion that one man differs from another"—he certainly would have admitted its truth. Mencken's belief in women's superiority resounds throughout *In Defense*. To reveal the inaccuracy of a number of stereotypes, Mencken proposes here "to set down in more or less plain form ideas that practically every civilized man and woman holds *in petto* [privately], but that have been concealed hitherto by the vast mass of sentimentalities swathing the whole woman question."[66] Woman's supposed intuition, Mencken explains, is really superior intelligence. Women are not idealists but rather "the supreme realists of the race."[67] More individualistic and less hypocritical than men, women rebel more often against convention. Men are more vain than women, and more cowardly. Mencken remarks appreciatively that women, unlike men, are growing less religious with the passage of time. In the end, the book's title is ironic, for women, as Mencken well knows, need no defense at all.

Mencken's destruction of these stereotypes, however, entertains the reader less than does the larger comic perspective into which Mencken places his subject. Cloaking his realism in burlesque, Mencken laughs uproariously at the grotesquely humorous efforts of men and women to deal with one another.

---

[65]Mencken, *A Mencken Chrestomathy*, 619.

[66]Mencken, *In Defense of Women* (Garden City, NY: Garden City Publishing Company, 1922) xiv-xv. All quotations are from this revised edition. For further discussion of Mencken and women, see Edward A. Martin, "H. L. Mencken and Equal Rights for Women," *Georgia Review* 35 (Spring 1981): 65–76; and the chapter of the same title in Martin's *H. L. Mencken and the Debunkers* (Athens, GA: University of Georgia Press, 1984) 47–59. See as well David Emblidge, "H. L. Mencken's *In Defense of Women*," *Menckeniana* 61 (Spring 1977): 5–10; Gwinn Owens, "Mencken on Women," *Menckeniana* 64 (Winter 1977): 2–3; and Vincent Fitzpatrick, "Wink Your Eye at Some Homely Girl: Misogyny and Mencken," *Menckeniana* 64 (Winter, 1977): 4–10.

[67]Mencken, *In Defense of Women*, 21.

Man's supposed attractiveness, Mencken explains, is "only the superficial splendor of a prancing animal." He uses even livelier analogies for the female form: "It has harsh curves and very clumsily distributed masses; compared to it the average milk-jug, or even cuspidor, is a things of intelligent and gratifying design." Men and women court with "solemn buffoonery," and marriage proves as much a matter of economics as of love. The boredom that sets in soon after marriage hardly bothers the average man: "He is weary when he gets home, and asks only the dull peace of a hog in a comfortable sty."[68] Unlike others who have written rancorously about men and women, or those long-suffering souls who have bled upon the page, Mencken wisely refuses to accuse or complain. He laughs instead and suggests that the most laudable individual is the one who acts with grace in the face of the most preposterous circumstances. Skillfully, Mencken makes his opponent's position all but indefensible. Who but the humorless, the unreflective, or the most sheltered would finally disagree?

The American Language, like *In Defense of Women*, developed from Mencken's earlier writing. Mencken had discussed philology in the Baltimore *Evening Sun* as early as 1910, and the *Smart Set* had published "The American: His Language" in 1913. Neither Alfred A. Knopf nor Mencken was optimistic about the book's reception, but when the first edition of *The American Language* appeared in March 1919, the 1,500 copies of the initial printing sold out quickly. Mencken was equally amazed by the enormity of the response to his request, in the preface, for contributions and suggestions. Mail poured in from a variety of sources, from scholars to interested lay people, and some letters ran to ten thousand words. This flow of material, along with Mencken's continuing scholarship, necessitated three more editions and two supplements. Philology held Mencken's interest longer than any other subject did; thirty-eight years

---

[68] Ibid., 35, 37, 58, 114.

elapsed between the appearance of his first newspaper piece and the publication of the second supplement.[69] In his subtitle, Mencken calls *The American Language* "a preliminary inquiry," and he proceeds to explain that the book pretends only "to articulate some of [its] materials—to get some approach to order and coherence into them, and so pave the way for work by some more competent man." Despite Mencken's disclaimer, this first edition offers more than three hundred pages of text, thoroughly documented, as well as a substantial bibliography and a long list of words and phrases. Combining narration and exposition, Mencken's nine chapters discuss such matters as pronunciation, honorifics, euphemism, vulgarity, spelling, proper names, and platitudes. The vernacular of *Huckleberry Finn* has puzzled the British. Similarly, when Charles Dickens's humor is presented through Cockney dialect such as Jeremy Cruncher's in *A Tale of Two Cities*, it has failed to delight a number of Americans. Perceiving differences such as these, Mencken uses the image of "diverging streams" to depict British and American English. These languages, "Mencken explains, "began to be recognizably different...in both vocabulary and punctuation by the opening of the nineteenth century," and he concludes that the streams have diverged even more with the passage of time.[70]

Although *The American Language* is distinguished by patient scholarship, it is lively and highly opinionated. Given Mencken's Anglophobia and his delight in the writing of Mark Twain, George Ade, and Ring Lardner, he understandably shows a preference for American English. He applauds its simplified spelling, verbal economy, greater malleability, and its propensity for neologism.

---

[69]Adler, *The Mencken Bibliography*, 9. Charles A. Fecher, *Mencken: A Study of His Thought* (New York: Knopf, 1978) 289. For further discussion, see Fecher, "The Philologian," in *Mencken: A Study of His Thought*, 289–309; and the scholarship of Dr. Raven I. McDavid, who edited an abridged version of *The American Language* and published prolifically on this matter.

[70]Mencken, *The American Language* (New York: Knopf, 1919) vi, 1, 63.

The American Language shows Mencken's unending fascination with the actual speech of living Americans: not what one hears in politicians' harangues or reads in highbrow magazines but rather what Otis and Hazeltine whisper as they court on the front porch and the speech employed at ball games and in bars. With obvious delight, Mencken captures such Americanisms as "he done himself proud," "it near finished him," and (perhaps Mencken appreciated this most) "he et hoggish."[71] The highly readable style and cohesive structure distinguish *The American Language* as much as its wealth of information does. Mencken at thirty-nine shows here, as he had failed to do the decade before with *Nietzsche*, the ability to make a complicated subject thoroughly accessible to a popular audience.

For *Prejudices: First Series*, which also appeared in 1919, Mencken again drew upon his previous writing, especially that in the *Smart Set*. This volume and the five that followed over the next eight years again show Mencken's peculiarly American style, for the books had to be translated for their English audience.[72] This series offers exactly what its title suggests, Mencken's prejudices, for the Baltimorean shows no inclination to present both sides of an issue. A substantial volume of 250 pages, *Prejudices: First Series* contains twenty-one chapters, nineteen of which are devoted to various forms of literature. This focus would change drastically during the next decade.

With "Criticism of Criticism of Criticism," the lead essay, Mencken provides one of his more informative discussions of aesthetics. Predictably, he embarrasses himself as a critic of poetry; he praises John Oppenheimer and Lizette Woodworth Reese (a Baltimorean) but disparages Edgar Lee Masters and Robert Frost. Turning to the theater, Mencken applauds George Jean Nathan but reverses his previous assessment of Shaw.

---

[71]Ibid., 227.
[72]Mencken to Vincent Starrett, 5 December 1938, in Forgue, *Letters*, 428–29.

Drawing upon the sententious Lord Chamberlain in *Hamlet*, Mencken dubs Shaw the "Ulster Polonius" and, in a much-quoted phrase, denigrates Shaw for announcing "the obvious in terms of the scandalous." Attacking the Irishman's "ethical obsession," Mencken suggests that Shaw has deteriorated from playwright to preacher. Similarly, Mencken changes his mind about H. G. Wells and Jack London, two novelists whom he had praised previously. In Mencken's eyes, these novelists, like Shaw, had lost their way. With Wells, Mencken laments "the absorption of the artist in the tin-pot reformer and professional wise man." Earlier, Mencken had applauded London's *The Call of the Wild* and *Martin Eden*, two mimetic novels, but when London decided to promote Temperance (he had a drinking problem) and socialism, Mencken could only complain that "the amateur Great Thinker" hampered London the writer of fiction.[73]

Mencken could hardly anticipate the direction that American life and literature would take. But for today's reader, gifted with hindsight, some of Mencken's judgments here contain a startling irony. Mencken could not foresee that his scorn for tendentious literature would cause him to be bludgeoned by radical critics and novelists during the 1930s. The critic who disparaged "the late Mr. Wells" could hardly predict that the same phrase would be applied to himself. Mencken, however, would experience his decade of greatest popularity before others dismissed him as cavalierly as he dismissed the English novelist.

Mencken's popularity during the 1920s would have been impossible without the many important developments during these eleven years from 1908 to 1919. With the publication of *Prefaces*, Mencken established himself as an unarguably major voice in American literary criticism. The other volumes appearing late in the decade enhanced his reputation as a philologian and social

---

[73]Mencken, "The Ulster Polonius," in *Prejudices: First Series*, 189. Mencken, "The Late Mr. Wells," in *Prejudices: First Series*, 29. Mencken, "Jack London," in *Prejudices: First Series*, 237.

critic. Much to his benefit, Mencken settled his publishing situation during these years; after 1918, Alfred A. Knopf would issue all of Mencken's books. As an editor, Mencken gained invaluable experience with the *Smart Set*; without this training, he could not have run the *American Mercury* with such expertise. In 1909, Mencken was first mentioned in a book by another author; by 1919, comments about the Baltimorean in books, magazines and newspapers filled several feet of shelves. The American reading public no longer had to ask, "Who's Mencken?"

Certainly, Mencken had exhibited the best of intentions when he wrote to Dreiser back in 1909. But in vowing to retrench, Mencken might just as well have promised to celebrate the virtues of the common citizen, to stop smoking his cigars, or to drink only one beer. Congenitally incapable of silence, Mencken, like Conrad's Kurtz, was blessed with the gift of the artist: he had something to say. During these eleven years, he had learned how to say it. Things would get far better before they got worse.

CHAPTER 4

The American Circus:
1920-1929

> This is the United States, God's favorite country. The
> fun of living here does not lie in playing chopping-block
> for the sanctified, but in outraging them and getting away
> with it. To this enterprise I address myself. Some day they
> may fetch me, but it will be a hard sweat.
> —*Mencken to Theodore Dreiser, 27 March [1921], in*
> Dreiser-Mencken Letters: The Correspondence of Theo-
> dore Dreiser and H. L. Mencken, 1907–1945

Robert Bridges, poet laureate of England for eleven years, came to
New York City in 1924. He was welcomed by a delegation from
the American Academy of Arts and Letters and was asked if he
wanted to meet anyone. "The only man I want to meet in
America," Bridges replied, "is H. L. Mencken." According to the
author Burton Rascoe, the delegation's response was such that
Bridges might just as well have said, "I am badly in need of a
whore. Will you please get me one for the night?"[1] Such an
encounter shows the extent to which the mere mention of
Mencken's name could affront the literary establishment and

---

[1]Sara Mayfield, *The Constant Circle: H. L. Mencken and His Friends* (New
York: Delacorte, 1968) 150. William Manchester, *Disturber of the Peace: The
Life of H. L. Mencken* (New York: Harper, 1950) 123.

attests to the extent of Mencken's reputation abroad. While Mencken had gained recognition in England, he acquired even more in America. The *New York Times* suggested that the Baltimorean was the most influential private citizen in the United States.[2] Mencken's popularity took a variety of forms, some more conventional than others. The first Mencken bibliography appeared in 1924, and the next year saw the publication of the first two books devoted entirely to his life and art. In addition, the periodical literature about Mencken increased even more appreciably than it had during the previous decade. The bibliophiles had discovered Mencken by this time and were collecting his early books. Hemingway referred to Mencken, albeit sardonically, in *The Torrents of Spring* and *The Sun Also Rises*, and F. Scott Fitzgerald took the opportunity to insert Mencken's name into the proofs of *This Side of Paradise*. Mencken even figured in the composition of *Gentlemen Prefer Blondes;* Anita Loos conceived of the book after she saw the middle-aged Mencken embarrassing himself with a frivolous young woman. (He applauded the book.)[3] College debating societies argued about the value of Mencken's writing, and some students took to flashing the Paris-green cover of the *American Mercury* as a badge of sophistication. Early in 1927, after several campus suicides were reported, one university president went so far as to set the cause as "too much Mencken." The Baltimorean took obvious delight in responding: "What I would like to see, if it could be arranged, would be a wave of suicides among college presidents.... A college student, leaping uninvited into the arms of God, pleases only himself. But a college president, doing the same thing, would give keen and permanent enjoyment to great

---

[2]Manchester, *Disturber of the Peace*, 158.
[3]*The New Mencken Letters*, ed. Carl Bode (New York: Dial Press, 1977) 552.

multitudes of persons." The president later resigned and entered the insurance business.[4]

The 1920s in America belonged more to Mencken than to any other single individual. Rarely have man and moment met so serendipitously. Mencken relished the follies of the democratic state—he saw democracy as "the art and science of running the circus from the monkey cage"—and the Harding administration generously provided the Teapot Dome scandal.[5] Forever amused by all messiahs, Mencken delighted in the antics of Billy Sunday and his kin. Mencken abhorred Prohibition—as a violation of his personal freedom, as a misguided attempt to legislate morality, and as a pathetic triumph of rural ignorance and Puritanism over urban sophistication—but as a writer he could hardly have been given a more convenient target. With its childlike optimism and its rowdy satisfactions, this decade eminently suited the writer who, by his own admission, had "a medieval but unashamed taste for the bizarre and indelicate [and a] congenital weakness for comedy of the grosser varieties."[6] With the war over and President Wilson in increasing disfavor, when the hemlines rose and many traditional values fell, America went on a spree. In 1925, F. Scott Fitzgerald chose the party, among other symbols in *The Great Gatsby*, to depict the American experience at this time.

Mencken chose a different image: "No other country houses so many gorgeous frauds and imbeciles as the United States.... I love this country as a small boy loves the circus." Like Walt Whitman, Mencken embraced multitudes. He thrust his arms wide, gathered in as much of American as possible, and made it all part of the show. Sometimes the president himself performed, albeit without vigor, in center ring: "Nero fiddled, but Coolidge only snored." In the side rings, lesser performers acted out the

---

[4]Mencken, "Under the Elms," in *A Mencken Chrestomathy* (New York: Knopf, 1949) 132–33.

[5]Mencken, *A Mencken Chrestomathy*, 622.

[6]Mencken, "On Being an American," in *Prejudices: Third Series* (New York: Knopf, 1922) 58.

fundamental banality and moronism of American life: "Lime and cement dealers being initiated into the Knight of Pythias, the Red Men or the Woodmen of the World.... Farmers plowing sterile fields behind sad, meditative horses, both suffering from the bites of insects.... Grocery clerks...trying to make assignations with soapy servant girls.... Wives and daughters of Middle Western country bankers, marooned in Los Angeles, going tremblingly to swami seances in dark, smelly rooms." Such acts seemed limitless, and for several years Mencken's audience applauded wildly at what he hawked as "incomparably the greatest show on earth."[7]

Far more than the two previous decades, the 1920s were distinguished by Mencken's mockery of the American scene. This is not to say that Mencken had avoided political and social criticism previously, nor is it to say that he now turned aside entirely from literary criticism. But Mencken definitely widened his focus during his forties, and this artistic decision, one of the most important of his career, profoundly affected his writing for books, magazines, and newspapers. More assertive as an editor, writing with even greater confidence, Mencken was denounced as the devil incarnate in the hinterlands and worshiped as a demigod in Boston. Mencken's shift of emphasis, however, was not without cost, and his increased notoriety could hardly last forever.

Written with George Jean Nathan, *The American Credo* appeared in 1920 and continued the productivity marking the end of the previous decade. Subtitled *A Contribution toward the Interpretation of the National Mind*, the book is divided into two sections. The latter, written by Nathan, offers 488 stereotypes to illustrate American superstition, provincialism, and imbecility. Mencken's preface of ninety-seven pages, another essay of monograph length, offers just as little optimism in setting forth the

---

[7]Mencken, "Statements of Belief II. Further 'Credos' of America's Living Authors," *Bookman* 68 (October 1928): 206–207. Mencken, "Coolidge," in *A Mencken Chrestomathy*, 253. Mencken, "Suite Americaine," in *Prejudices: Third Series*, 321–22. Mencken, "On Being an American," 58.

truth about "the great masses of simple men." Bemoaning the
American lust for conformity, Mencken alludes to Daniel Defoe
by remarking that in "no other country in the world is there so
ferocious a short way with dissenters; in none other is it socially so
costly to heed the inner voice and be one's own man." In attacking
the mentality of the mob—its suspicion, cowardice, and delight in
cruel spectacles such as lynching—Mencken resembles Colonel
Sherburn in *Huckleberry Finn*. The gullible American, Mencken
explains, is easily duped by advertisers. With his lack of respect
for liberty, the American fails to discuss sex and politics openly
and allows himself to be cowed by religion: "Save in a few large
cities, every American community lies under a sacerdotal
despotism, whose devices are disingenuous and dishonorable."
Blindly ambitious, the American becomes a tawdry social climber.
Moreover, Mencken remarks at some length, the contemporary
American endorses morality rather than honor. This morality
compels him to see all issues as either right or wrong and to act
officiously toward his neighbors. The honorable person, on the
other hand, keeps his promises, loathes excuses, and minds his
own business. Lamenting America's lack of stable tradition,
Mencken goes so far as to draw his native land as a
"ship...eternally at sea. Money vanishes, official dignity is
forgotten, caste lines are as full of gaps as an ill-kept hedge. The
grandfather of the Vanderbilts was a bounder; the last of the
Washingtons is a petty employee of the Library of Congress."[8]

Mencken's mentality obviously differed from the "national
mind." Mencken's desire to be left alone conflicted with society's
desire to regulate the lives of its private citizens. Like the
traditionalist farmer in Robert Frost's "Mending Wall," Mencken
believed absolutely that good fences make good neighbors.
Mencken believed that people do the most good by taking care of

---

[8]Mencken and George Jean Nathan, *The American Credo: A Contribution
toward the Interpretation of the National Mind* (New York: Knopf, 1920) 9,
41–42, 45, 32.

themselves and the people for whom they are responsible. Mencken openly admitted that his political views were based not upon altruism but rather upon self-interest. At the beginning of his great decade, Mencken made his beliefs clear: this artist would dispute the settled beliefs of his native land.

In the remaining five volumes of the *Prejudices* series, which appeared from 1920 to 1927, inclusive, Mencken continued this focus upon the American scene. As he had done in the series' first volume, Mencken drew upon material that had appeared previously and offered it again with various degrees of revision. His format, as he explained to a correspondent in 1920, was "a fundamental structure of serious argument, with enough personal abuse to engage the general, and one or two Rabelaisian touches."[9] As time passed, Mencken assigned Rabelais a larger part.

Offering abrasive commentary as well as humor, *Prejudices: Second Series* moves easily between the serious and the absurd. Once again, Mencken attacks Puritanism, censorship, and Woodrow Wilson. In "The Dry Millennium," he denounces Prohibition. In his ironically entitled "The Cult of Hope," Mencken derides America's lust for reformers, those "chronic hopers of the world, the believers in men, ideas, and things. These are the advocates of leagues of nations, wars to make the world safe for democracy, political mountebanks [and] 'clean-up' campaigns." The American mentality is too unrealistic, Mencken complains, to admit that many of life's problems are insoluble. In a lighter vein, he devotes a lengthy chapter, "Appendix on a Tender Theme," to romantic love, in which he echoes *In Defense of Women:* "It is, in brief, a wholesale diminishing of disgusts [that] often, in its later stages, [takes] on an hallucinatory and pathological character."[10]

---

[9]Mencken to Fielding Hudson Garrison, 4 November 1920, in *Letters of H. L. Mencken*, ed. Guy J. Forge (New York: Knopf, 1961) 207.

[10]Mencken, "The Cult of Hope," in *Prejudices: Second Series* (New York: Knopf, 1920) 213. Mencken, "Appendix on a Tender Theme," in *Prejudices: Second Series*, 229.

While they differ markedly in technique, both the first and last chapters in *Prejudices: Third Series* strongly indict the American way. "On Being an American," the volume's lead essay, runs to fifty-six pages and offers some rollicking Menckenese. "Here," he proclaims, "the general average of intelligence, of knowledge, of competence, of integrity, of self-respect, of honor is so low that any man who knows his trade, does not fear ghosts, has read fifty good books and practices the common decencies stands out as brilliantly as a wart on a bald head." After detailing the ease of life in "this glorious commonwealth of morons," Mencken attacks the American's prudery, fear of ideas, misguided Anglophilia, and yearning for extravagant religious rituals. Politics in America, Mencken laments, never proceeds beyond low comedy. "Suite Americaine," a provocative chapter of only fives pages, concludes the volume by sketching the American's homely aspirations, dubious virtues, and false claims of eminence. Some of Mencken's vignettes are droll: "Pastors of one-horse little churches in decadent villages, who, whenever when they drink two cups of coffee at supper, dream all night that they have been elected bishops." Others show pathos: "Women confined for the ninth or tenth time, wondering helplessly what it is all about."[11] While America certainly made Mencken laugh, the barbaric morality that generated so much needless suffering also made him sigh helplessly.

Mencken's censure continues in *Prejudices: Fourth Series*, where the lead essay, "The American Tradition," argues once again that the true American heritage is marked by revolt and individualism rather than by acquiescence and conformity. Bludgeoning the Anglo-Saxon mentality, Mencken says that the "normal American of the 'pure-blooded' majority goes to bed every night with an uneasy feeling that there is a burglar under the

---

[11]Mencken, "On Being an American," in *Prejudices: Third Series* (New York: Knopf, 1922) 13, 18. Mencken, "Suite Americaine," in *Prejudices: Third Series*, 320, 322.

bed, and he gets up every morning with a sickening fear that his underwear has been stolen." Mencken writes no more kindly about America's elected officials—"a good politician, under democracy, is quite as unthinkable as an honest burglar"—and its farmers. The husbandman, Mencken snorts, hates the city man and takes every opportunity to gouge him but then hollers for help when prices fall. Inhabiting America's dark prairies of fear and intolerance, the farmer opposes culture and freedom of expression: "There, where the cows low through the still night, and the jug of Peruna [a patent medicine taken as a tonic] stands beside the stove, and bathing begins...with the equinox—there is the reservoir of all the nonsensical legislation which now makes the United States a buffoon among the great nations."[12] Here, as elsewhere in his canon, Mencken has no romantic vision about life on the land.

Quantitatively, *Prejudices: Sixth Series* reverses the focus upon literature marking the series' first volume eight years before. Mencken attacks several long-standing enemies: chiropractors ("Dives into Quackery"), metaphysicians, and pedagogues. In his lengthy second chapter, subtitled "Government by Bounder," Mencken deplores the growth of democracy in America and the attendant decline in personal freedom and respect for the Bill of Rights. In "The Libido for the Ugly," containing his famous description of the landscape near Pittsburgh, Mencken speaks of a place "so dreadfully hideous, so intolerably bleak and forlorn that it reduced the whole aspiration of man to a macabre and depressing joke." Mencken uses such hideousness as a point of departure to decry the American "love of ugliness for its own sake, the lust to make the world intolerable.... Out of the melting pot emerges a race which hates beauty as much as it hates truth."[13] Mencken thereby offers a revisionist treatment, a decidedly

---

[12]Mencken, "The American Tradition," in *Prejudices: Fourth Series* (New York: Knopf, 1924) 39. Mencken, "The Politician," in *Prejudices: Fourth Series*, 130. Mencken, "The Husbandman," in *Prejudices: Fourth Series*, 54.

[13]Mencken, "The Libido for the Ugly," in *Prejudices: Sixth Series* (New York: Knopf, 1927) 187, 193.

negative one, of the melting-pot myth that others have used to speak so grandiosely of the possibilities of America. Appropriately, *Prejudices: Sixth Series* concludes with Mencken's discussion of the American West, that land at the end of Walt Whitman's open road. By this time in American history, however, the American frontier had been closed for decades, and Mencken does not echo Whitman's sense of promise, nor does Mencken view the "territory" as appreciatively as Huck Finn does at the end of that provocative novel bearing his name. Instead, Mencken laughs at the American film industry, which he found garish, in a chapter memorably entitled "Appendix from Moronia."

"Moronia," a lively neologism, serves as an appropriate final term for the title of Mencken's final chapter in *Prejudices*. Taking full advantage of the series' malleability, Mencken ranges in form from the aphorism to the essay, in tone from contumely to burlesque, and in subject matter from the banal aspiration of youth to the settled ignorance of age. These final five volumes of *Prejudices* present, at considerable length, Mencken's quarrel with his native land and show his immense delight in stirring up the animals all across America.

He took equal delight in his writing for newspapers, and his columns, more often than not, showed similar gusto. Mencken's reputation as a journalist reached its height during this decade and the early part of the 1930s; he was viewed as America's foremost newspaperman.[14] Such fame was attributable in part to Mencken's first syndicated column. From November 1924 until January 1928, he wrote about 160 pieces for the *Chicago Sunday Tribune*. Mencken's columns appeared in fifteen states as well as in India, Japan, China, England, and New Zealand. They did not always run without incident. "I started out by discussing relatively safe literary matters," Mencken explained later, "but soon got into

---

[14]Carl Bode, *Mencken* (Carbondale IL: Southern Illinois University Press, 1969) 202.

politics and religion, and some of the articles caused violent local uproars, and forced harassed editors to suspend the series."[15]

Some of these syndicated pieces appeared as "Monday Articles" in the Baltimore *Evening Sun*. Running from 1920 to 1938, the longest appearance for any of Mencken's columns, these pieces contained some of his more accomplished and memorable journalism. Even though these "Monday Articles" have not appeared for more than sixty years, they still generate comment among Baltimore's older citizens. Apparently, many Baltimoreans were in the habit of reading Monday's *Evening Sun* backwards. They would open to the editorial page first and wonder, "What's Mencken up to this week?"

As Mencken explained to Paul Patterson, the president and publisher of the *Sunpapers*, the newspaper had no obligation to serve as "a court of justice." Mencken argued that "when a scoundrel is on the block he ought to be denounced in plain terms, and without any judicial tenderness. So with fools. So with fool ideas."[16] He followed his own advice. He wrote, for example, several vitriolic columns about lynchings on Maryland's Eastern Shore, an area that he viewed as shamefully unreconstructed. These columns generated the expected caustic editorial mail and rebuttals, but they also led to talk of a boycott of the *Sunpapers* as well as to threats that Mencken would not be wise to cross the Chesapeake Bay.[17]

"The Carnival of Buncombe," Mencken's first "Monday Article," dealt with the presidential aspirants and left no doubt as to what would follow. In January 1921, Mencken used the same trope in entitling his column about the United States House of Representatives "The Asses' Carnival." In March of that same

[15]Mencken, "HLM," EPFL. Quoted by Betty Adler, *H. L. M.: The Mencken Bibliography* (Baltimore: Johns Hopkins University Press, 1961) 108.

[16]Mencken to Paul Patterson, 12 July [1928], in Bode, *The New Mencken Letters*, 223.

[17]These columns ran in 1931 and 1933. See Adler, *The Mencken Bibliography*, 76, 78.

year, Mencken seized the opportunity to comment upon the style of President Harding's inaugural address, which the Baltimorean had been forced to endure in Washington. The previous decade, in an observation that has gained just acclaim, Mencken had lampooned the writing of Thorstein Veblen, author of *The Theory of the Leisure Class*, as the "self-evident made horrifying, the obvious in terms of the staggering. Marx, I daresay, said a good deal of it…. But Marx, at this business, labored under a technical handicap: he wrote in German, a language he actually understood. Prof. Dr. Veblen submits himself to no such disadvantage."[18] Mencken's readers at the time could hardly have been faulted if they had concluded that Mencken would never surpass such devastating irony, but President Harding's platitudes generated an even more rollicking satire. In "Gamalielese," a spoof on Harding's middle name, Mencken concluded that "setting aside a college professor or two and half a dozen dipsomaniacal newspaper reporters…he writes the worst English that I have ever encountered. It reminds me of a string of wet sponges; it reminds me of tattered washing on the line; it reminds me of stale bean soup, of college yells, of dogs barking idiotically through endless nights."[19] Only a skeptic with no innate respect for America's highest elected official and a writer blessed with such a fertile imagination could have written so effectively. His expertise is so pronounced here that it seems almost unfair.

Turning the next year from Harding to alcohol, Mencken called another column "The Boozeart," and in 1923 America's overcrowded schools generated "Educational Rolling Mills." For these "Monday Articles," however, Mencken did not always draw

---

[18]Mencken, "A Carnival of Buncombe," Baltimore *Evening Sun*, 9 February 1920. Mencken, "The Asses' Carnival," Baltimore *Evening Sun*, 31 January 1921. Mencken, "Professor Veblen," in *Prejudices: First Series* (New York: Knopf, 1919) 66.

[19]Mencken, "Gamalielese," Baltimore *Evening Sun*, 7 March 1921. See George Douglas, *H. L. Mencken: Critic of American Life* (Hamden, CT: Archon Books, 1978) 143–49.

upon such garish public spectacles as the incoherence of the President, the ridiculousness of Prohibition, or the futility of mass education. Always resourceful, forever relishing the absurd, Mencken found material in places that a less imaginative journalist would have ignored. One spring day, for example, he looked out of his study on Hollins Street and saw agents of the Salvation Army and the YMCA setting up for a ceremony on the lawn of Union Square across the street. His curiosity piqued, Mencken watched attentively, and his "Sunday Afternoon" reduced the best efforts of these sanctimonious souls to slapstick. Every pious individual wanted to be the boss and shouted contradictory orders; the truck was driven six feet forward and then moved the same distance back. Obviously more skilled at prayer than at the mundane task of unloading planks for the stage, the men whacked one another across their backsides. They built a stage so unsteady that the terrified children, who had the good sense to see what their elders could not, had to be herded onto it and then be quickly removed before it toppled onto the soft grass. Mencken expressed no surprise. "I present the record," he concluded typically, "as a small contribution to the literature of human imbecility."[20]

Mencken made a far larger contribution to this literature through his commentary upon events in Dayton, Tennessee, during July 1925. In March of that year, the Tennessee legislature had passed the Butler Bill, which made it unlawful for any instructor in a school publicly funded "to teach any theory that denies the story of the Divine Creation of man as taught in the Bible, and to teach instead that man has descended from a lower order of the animals."[21] The next month, John Scopes, a high-school science

[20]Mencken, "The Boozeart," Baltimore *Evening Sun*, 11 December 1922. Mencken, "Educational Rolling Mills," Baltimore *Evening Sun*, 16 April 1923. Mencken, "Sunday Afternoon," Baltimore *Evening Sun*, 1 April 1929.

[21]Arthur Garfield Hays, *Let Freedom Ring* (New York: Boni, 1928) 25. For an excellent discussion of Mencken's motivation and the role of the Baltimore *Sunpapers* in the Scopes trial, see S. L. Harrison, "Anatomy of the Scopes Trial: Mencken's Media Event," *Menckeniana* 135 (Fall 1995): 1–6. For more detailed

teacher and football coach, volunteered to test the law and was subsequently arrested. William Jennings Bryan, who nearly thirty years before had offered his impassioned "Cross of Gold" speech and had more recently served as the Secretary of State, volunteered from Florida to serve as the prosecuting attorney. The American Civil Liberties Union in New York City sent Dudley Field Malone and Arthur Garfield Hays. Mencken suggested that Clarence Darrow, the prominent attorney who had defended Leopold and Loeb during their highly publicized murder trial the year before, also be engaged. "Nobody gives a damn about that yap schoolteacher," Mencken told Darrow. "The thing to do is make a fool out of Bryan."[22] The Baltimore *Sunpapers* posted Scopes's bond (and would later pay his hundred dollar fine, which was subsequently rescinded) and sent five men, a cartoonist and four columnists including Mencken, to cover the show. Mencken's dispatches ran in the Financial edition of the *Evening Sun*; he also drew upon the uproar in Dayton for several "Monday Articles." Mencken's dispatches were syndicated in the South and gave the Baltimorean and the *Sunpapers* immense notoriety in this highly publicized battle between science and religion, this timeless struggle, as Mencken saw things, between knowledge and superstition.[23]

Given Mencken's attitudes, it is hardly surprising that the events in Dayton would alternately delight and disgust him. He would find it impossible to take seriously a trial that opened each day with a prayer. He could only guffaw at locals such as the figure who wore a sandwich board proclaiming him the Bible champion of the world and at the atheist who paraded a mangy chimpanzee through the town. On the other hand, Mencken complained stridently that an event such as the Scopes trial could

---

discussions of Mencken and the Scopes trial, see Manchester, *Disturber of the Peace*, 160–86; Mayfield, *The Constant Circle*, 87–91; Bode, *Mencken*, 264–70; and Fred Hobson, *Mencken: A Life* (New York: Random House, 1994) 256–60.

[22]Manchester, *Disturber of the Peace*, 164.

[23]See Adler, *H. L. M.: The Mencken Bibliography*, 98–99.

happen in a supposedly civilized country during the twentieth century. Before he left Baltimore, Mencken wrote columns entitled "The Tennessee Circus" and "Homo Neandertalensis." Modern science and "the ancient Hebrew demonology," he argued, could never be reconciled, and the religious organizations attacking the teaching of evolution were "nothing more, at bottom, than conspiracies of the inferior man against his betters." It was with strong opinions, and great expectations, that Mencken began his pilgrimage to the "hills of Zion."[24]

Once he arrived in Dayton, Mencken called the town "a universal joke" and lamented that a verdict of guilty was inevitable. "To call a man a doubter in these parts," Mencken snorted, "is to accuse him of cannibalism."[25] Mencken was merely warming up for his dispatch of July 13, where he recounted an evening spent with the Holy Rollers in the hills outside Dayton. Mencken witnessed someone denouncing the reading of all books except the Bible, and then he saw a young girl fling herself onto the ground:

---

[24]Mencken, "The Tennessee Circus," Baltimore *Evening Sun*," 15 June 1925. Mencken "Homo Neandertalensis," Baltimore *Evening Sun*, 29 June 1925. Mencken used "The Hills of Zion" as the title for the revised version of his dispatch of July 13 from Dayton; in *Prejudices, Fifth Series* (New York: Knopf, 1926) 75-86, reprinted in *A Mencken Chrestomathy*, 392–98. "Homo Neandertalensis" and Mencken's dispatches from Dayton are included in the invaluable *The Impossible H. L. Mencken: A Selection of His Best Newspaper Stories*, ed. Marion Elizabeth Rodgers (New York: Doubleday, 1991) 562–611. Mencken also wrote winningly about Dayton in the material that he consigned to time lock; see *Thirty-Five Years of Newspaper Work: A Memoir by H. L. Mencken*, ed. Fred Hobson, Vincent Fitzpatrick, and Bradford Jacobs (Baltimore: Johns Hopkins University Press, 1992) 136–149.

[25]Mencken, "Mencken Finds Daytonians Full of Sickening Doubts About the Value of Publicity," Baltimore *Evening Sun*, 9 July 1925. Mencken, "Impossibility of Obtaining a Fair Trial Insure Scopes' Conviction, Says Mencken," Baltimore *Evening Sun*, 10 July 1925. Mencken, "Mencken Likens Trial to Religious Orgy, with Defense a Beelzebub," Baltimore *Evening Sun*, 11 July 1925.

What followed quickly reached such heights of
barbaric grotesquerie that it was hard to believe it real. At
a signal all the faithful crowded up the bench and began to
pray—not in unison but each for himself. At another they
fell on their knees, their arms over the penitent. The leader
kneeled, facing us, his head alternately thrown back
dramatically or buried in his hands. Words spouted from
his lips liked bullets from a machine gun—appeals to pull
the penitent back out of hell, defiances of the powers and
principalities of the air, a vast impassioned jargon of
apocalyptic texts…. The climax was a shrill, inarticulate
squawk, like that of a man throttled. He fell back headlong
across the heap of supplicants.

A comic scene? Somehow, no. The poor half-wits
were too horribly in earnest. It was like peeping through a
knothole at the writhings of people in pain. From the
squirming and jabbering mass a young woman gradually
detached herself—a woman not uncomely, with a pathetic
homemade cap on her head. Her head jerked back, the
veins of her neck swelled, and her fists went to her throat
as if she were fighting for breath. She bent backward until
she was like half a hoop. Then she suddenly snapped
forward. We caught a flash of the whites of her eyes.
Presently her whole body began to be convulsed…. She
would leap to her feet, thrust her arms in the air and then
hurl herself upon the heap.[26]

Such were the fruits of nearly 150 years of American civilization.
Under the spell of Mencken's narrative here, one all but expects
the devil to rise out of the ground and proclaim that he has won,

---

[26]Mencken, "Yearning Mountaineers' Souls Need Reconversion Nightly,
Mencken Finds," Baltimore *Evening Sun*, 13 July 1925; quoted at greater length
by Manchester, *Disturber of the Peace*, 176–77. See note 24.

that a symbolic darkness has claimed all the land. Mencken was denied the luxury of recollecting such emotion in tranquility. Working under the pressure of a deadline and stripped to his underwear, he wrote this entrancing copy in a sweltering hotel room. When the dispatch reached the *Sunpapers*, an editor tacked it onto a bulletin board and announced, "That's reporting."[27] Further commentary would have been superfluous.

As the case wore on, Mencken continued to place the proceedings in the larger contexts of free speech and governmental interference with the rights of its citizens. The people in Dayton, Mencken observed, were no more free to make up their own minds than American citizens had been before America entered World War I. Moreover, Mencken stepped up his assaults on Bryan: *ad hominem* attacks, criticism of his theology, and mockery of the futility of his career. "Once he had one leg in the White House," the Baltimorean scoffed, "and the nation trembled under his roars. Now he is a tinpot pope in the coca-cola belt." On July 18, in his final dispatch, Mencken warned his readers not to dismiss the trial as a farce; other states were hardly immune to such proceedings.[28]

His work back home was piling up, and Mencken returned to Baltimore after the judge refused to admit the testimony of expert witnesses called by the defense. Consequently, Mencken was absent when Darrow called Bryan to the stand and the Great Commoner thundered that man is not a mammal. Bryan died of a stroke on July 26. Tennessee Governor Austin Peay said that Bryan had died "a martyr to the faith of our fathers" and proclaimed a state holiday.[29] Mencken disagreed. In his "Bryan,"

[27]Manchester, *Disturber of the Peace*, 177.

[28]Mencken, "Malone the Victor, Even Though Court Sides with Opponents, Mencken Says," Baltimore *Evening Sun*, 17 July 1925. Mencken, "Battle Over Now, Mencken Sees; Genesis Triumphant and Ready for New Jousts," Baltimore *Evening Sun*, 18 July 1925.

[29]Edward J. Larson, *Summer for the Gods: The Scopes Trial and America's Continuing Debate Over Science and Religion* (New York, Basic Books, 1997) 203. See Vincent Fitzpatrick, *Gerald W. Johnson: From Southern Liberal to*

which ran the next day in the *Evening Sun*, Mencken obviously scorned the Latin maxim *de mortuis nil nisi bonum* (say only good things about the dead), and the column was strikingly cruel. More than once, Mencken became needlessly personal—the harping upon Bryan's ugliness, for example—in his censure of the deceased. He likened Bryan to a rabid dog that "bit right and left" and said that "he came into life a hero, a Galahad in bright and shining armor. Now he is passing out a pathetic fool." Mencken concluded that "he seemed only a poor clod like those around him, deluded by a childish theology, full of an almost pathological hatred of all learning, all human dignity, all beauty, all fine and noble things. He was a peasant come home to the dung pile." Later, when he revised and expanded the column, Mencken grew even more caustic. Reducing Bryan to images of dirt, grease, sweat, and excrement, Mencken made his opponent seem scarcely human. "In Memoriam: W. J. B." proved as much a forceful indictment of rural America as an ironic elegy of a person whom Mencken despised. Bryan's "baroque theology," Mencken argued at length, appealed not to the intelligent but rather to the ignorant and superstitious—that is, to those of arrested evolutionary development.[30]

While Mencken loathed the encroachment of religion upon secular matters, he finally had to be grateful, as a journalist, for the opportunities that the Tennessee legislature had offered him. He reveled in the cast of characters, from the prosecuting attorney to the itinerant preacher who filled Dayton, in the events of the trial, and in the extracurricular activities in the hills beyond. All of these stood together as an objective correlative of the American mentality that Mencken found so patently offensive: its lust for cheap theatrics, its provincial fear of learning, its assent to

---

National Conscience (Baton Rouge: Louisiana State University Press, 2002) 74–76.

[30]Mencken, "Bryan," Baltimore *Evening Sun*, 27 July 1925. Mencken, "In Memoriam: W. J. B.," in *A Mencken Chrestomathy* (New York: Knopf, 1949) 243–48.

ignorance and superstition, and its lack of respect for the law. Finally, the Scopes trial was, like Prohibition, a windfall for Mencken.[31] Of all his journalism, these columns about the Tennessee circus remain the best known. Less than a year after he left the hills of Zion, Mencken found himself involved in another trial, this one in Boston, over freedom of speech. The *New York Times* reported this confrontation involving the *American Mercury* as a "second Scopes trial."[32] Just as Mencken's acerbic comments about the events in Dayton caused him to be bludgeoned in the Southern press, the *Mercury* was banned periodically in rural Southern communities.[33] Mencken's editing of this magazine clearly added to the controversy by his books and journalism. He was called a "putrid, public pest" who ran the periodical that posed "the greatest single danger in American life."[34] While the Scopes trial is the single event with which Mencken is most frequently associated, the *American Mercury* is the publication with which his name is most often linked. In fact, "Mencken" and "the *Mercury*" became all but synonymous. This coupling marked one of the magazine's greatest strengths as well as a significant factor in its decline.

---

[31]Manchester, *Disturber of the Peace*, 173.
[32]"Judge Reads Piece in Mencken Case," *New York Times*, 7 April 1926, 25. Quoted by Robert F. Nardini, "Mencken and the 'Cult of Smartness,'" *Menckeniana* 84 (Winter 1982): 4–5.
[33]M. K. Singleton, *H. L. Mencken and the "American Mercury" Adventure* (Durham, NC: Duke University Press, 1962) 167. This book offers a detailed history of the magazine. For another valuable history, see Frank Luther Mott, *A History of American Magazines*, vol. 5 of *Sketches of 21 Magazines, 1905–1930*, 26. The *Mercury* finally ceased publication in 1980 with no notice of cessation. For an account of the magazine from its inception to its demise, see Vincent Fitzpatrick, "*The American Mercury*," in *American Literary Magazines: The Twentieth Century*, ed. Edward E. Chielens (Westport, CT: Greenwood Press, 1992) 7–16.
[34]Mencken, *Menckeniana: A Schimpflexikon* (New York: Knopf, 1928) 65, 70.

Several issues influenced Mencken's decision to leave the *Smart Set* and establish this new periodical that gave him greater latitude as both an editor and a critic. From the time that he and Nathan began to edit the *Smart Set* in 1914, Mencken was dissatisfied with its title, cover, and readership. Unable to reshape the magazine as he wished, Mencken grew increasingly exasperated. Also, the *Smart Set*, as primarily a magazine of fiction, was hardly a suitable forum for Mencken's increasing interest in social criticism. Moreover, by 1923, Mencken had convinced himself that he no longer needed to battle the censors. He concluded, quite incorrectly, that they now lacked the power to suppress a book of consequence.[35] (Four years later, Dreiser's *An American Tragedy* was banned in Boston.) Despite Mencken's dissatisfaction with the magazine, his changing interests, and the periodical's decline in sales, he and Nathan were still willing to continue the *Smart Set* as an all-fiction counterpart to the *American Mercury*. However, Eltinge Warner, the publisher, made this impossible. In 1914, Warner had agreed to keep out of the *Smart Set*'s editorial affairs, but he broke his promise in 1923. After President Harding's death in August, Mencken and Nathan planned to run a satirical story on his funeral train. Warner forbade its publication, and the editors resigned as of the December issue.[36]

The *American Mercury*'s first issue appeared in January 1924. Mencken and Nathan each owned one-sixth of the stock—the remaining were divided among Alfred A. Knopf, his wife, and his father—and exercised full editorial control.[37] The *Mercury* was intended for the intelligent, solvent, urbane

---

[35]Mencken, "Fifteen Years," *Smart Set* 72 (December 1923): 141.

[36]Carl Richard Dolmetsch, "Mencken as Magazine Editor," *Menckeniana* 21 (Spring 1967): 7. Carl Richard Dolmetsch, "'HLM' and "GJN': The Editorial Partnership Re-Examined," *Menckeniana* 75 (Fall 1980): 35. Mott, *A History of American Magazines*, 270.

[37]Alfred A. Knopf, "H. L. Mencken, George Jean Nathan, and the *American Mercury* Adventure," *Menckeniana* 78 (Summer 1981): 5.

American who looked askance at such things as democracy, Prohibition, and the yearning to save humanity. *"The American Mercury* will never have a million circulation," Mencken explained its editorial policy. "It is not headed in that direction. Its function is to depict America for the wholly enlightened sort of Americans—realistically, with good humor, and wholly without cant. Its aim is to entertain that minority—and give it consolation."[38] Nobody, at least for several years, found the magazine dull.

Moreover, few found it unattractive. As Mencken wished, the magazine's rambunctious content was decorously clothed by the distinguished Paris-green cover and sedate title. "What we need," Mencken wrote to Theodore Dreiser, who had suggested several flashy titles for the magazine, "is something that looks highly respectable outwardly. The American Mercury will be almost perfect for that purpose. What will go on inside the tent is another story. You will recall that the late P. T. Barnum got away with burlesque shows by calling them moral lectures."[39] The *Mercury*'s paper was expensive Scotch featherweight, and its attractive Garamond type was set in double columns. Each issue of 128 pages carried no illustrations.[40] Mencken and Nathan now had a magazine whose understated elegance set it apart from many of its competitors.

While Mencken and Nathan carried over from the *Smart Set* their columns on books and the theater, they also continued to handle submissions as they had previously. The approval of both editors was necessary for a manuscript to be accepted; authors

---

[38]Mencken, "Postscript," in *Three Years, 1924–1927: The Story of a New Idea and Its Successful Adaptation* by Earl Bachman, et al. (New York: *American Mercury*, 1927) 35–36.

[39]Mencken to Theodore Dreiser, 10 September [1923], in *Dreiser-Mencken Letters: The Correspondence of Theodore Dreiser and H. L. Mencken, 1907–1945*, 2 volumes, ed. Thomas P. Riggio (Philadelphia: University of Pennsylvania Press) 502.

[40]Singleton, *H. L. Mencken and the* American Mercury *Adventure*, 39–40.

received a quick response to their material as well as payment upon acceptance rather than upon publication. Moreover, after a piece appeared, its copyright was transferred to the author. These editorial courtesies helped to compensate for the magazine's low rate of pay: the *Mercury* offered only two cents a word for prose contributions.[41]

As an editor, Mencken benefitted from his wide network of contacts, his absolute lack of prejudice about people, and his flair for the unexpected. While such prominent literary figures as Theodore Dreiser, F. Scott Fitzgerald, Sherwood Anderson, Sinclair Lewis, and Edgar Lee Masters appeared in the *Mercury*, so did Margaret Mead the anthropologist, Emma Goldman the political radical, and Margaret Sanger the advocate of birth control. Both realist and civil libertarian, Mencken believed that "so few men are really worth knowing that it is seems a shameful waste to let an anthropoid prejudice stand in the way of free association with one who is." Among African-American writers and public figures, George Schuyler, Langston Hughes, Countee Cullen, James Weldon Johnson, and W. E. B. Du Bois wrote for the magazine.[42] Moreover, Mencken succeeded in acquiring material from a variety of figures not actively courted by other magazines. Convicts, hoboes, and dishwashers contributed to the *Mercury*, as did taxi drivers and outdoorsmen. The magazine remained open to journalists—Mencken ran several pieces by his colleagues on the *Sunpapers*—as well as to academic critics. The eclectic nature of its contributors proved one of the *Mercury's* greatest strengths.

---

[41]Ibid., 37.

[42]Mencken, "The Library," *American Mercury* 23 (May 1931): 125. Quoted by Fenwick Anderson, "Black Perspectives in Mencken's *Mercury*," *Menckeniana* 70 (Summer1979): 3. See Anderson's informative essay for discussions of the black writers who appeared in the magazine and the *Mercury's* treatment of racial matters. See as well Charles Scruggs, *The Sage in Harlem: H. L. Mencken and the Black Writers of the 1920s* (Baltimore: Johns Hopkins University Press, 1984) 68–77.

The magazine's nonfiction, as well as some of its more celebrated features, tended to be satirical. In fact, more than one-third of the essays published between 1924 and 1929 ridiculed some aspect of the American scene. The more vulnerable targets were assaulted repeatedly: pedagogy, chiropractic, Christian Science, Prohibition, Puritanism, and the sad credulity of rural America.[43] "Americana," a feature continued from the *Smart Set*, offered items gleaned from newspapers and magazines all across the land. Determined to show the imbecility of the American mind, Mencken and Nathan did not lack material. Truth proved more damning than fiction, for the items in "Americana" offered an even bleaker picture of life in the United States than did the stereotypes that Nathan had concocted for *The American Credo*. For example, the *Mercury* recounted the story of the young man in Oregon who, believing that fasting would improve his health, died of starvation. And here was the sad tale of the wife who divorced her husband because, at the breakfast table, he drank his milk directly from a goat's udder. The irreverence of "Americana" so incensed George Horace Lorimer, the editor of the *Saturday Evening Post*, that he instituted a reciprocal feature to show the more positive aspects of the American scene. Apparently, Lorimer had more trouble finding material than Mencken and Nathan did, for this feature disappeared from the *Saturday Evening Post*.[44]

The initial printing of the *Mercury*'s first issue was five thousand; a second printing was necessary, then a third. In all, the January 1924 *Mercury* sold more than 15,000 copies and far surpassed the most optimistic expectations. While the magazine cost fifty cents, some copies of the first issue sold for as much as fifty dollars. By the end of the year, circulation had climbed past

---

[43]Singleton, *H. L. Mencken and the* American Mercury *Adventure*, 55–110.

[44]These "Americana" columns for February 1924 and July 1925 are cited by Gerald Schwartz, "The West as Gauged by H. L. Mencken's *American Mercury*," *Menckeniana* 89 (Spring 1984): 2–3. For Lorimer's response to Mencken, see H. Alan Wycherley, "'Americana': The Mencken-Lorimer Feud," *Costerus* 5 (1972): 227–36.

42,000. Nathan resigned as co-editor in 1925—he found his continuing interest in the fine arts, particularly in the theater, incompatible with Mencken's larger focus—but his departure had no noticeable impact. By December 1925 circulation had surpassed 62,000.[45] The spring of 1926 was marked by the uproar over Herbert Asbury's "Hatrack," an essay that appeared in the April issue. Arthur Garfield Hays, one of the lawyers who had assisted with the defense of John Scopes, helped to defend the *Mercury* in this most important censorship case involving Mencken the magazine editor. Containing relatively little controversial material, "Hatrack" was the catalyst for a trial that brought Mencken and his magazine much notoriety and a subsequent series of events that, most probably, led Mencken to reconsider his conclusions about the strength of censorship in America.

A chapter from Asbury's forthcoming *Up from Methodism*, "Hatrack" is set in Farmington, Missouri. Asbury criticizes the Midwestern evangelists who denounce harlotry in order to gain attention for themselves; then, he attacks the prurience of small town life. His central character is a skinny, credulous domestic servant who envisions herself a model and moonlights as a prostitute. Hatrack devotedly attends not only the church services on Sunday but also the numerous meetings and revivals. She is scorned, however, by the supposed Christians who ignore Christ's command to love one's neighbor as oneself. After being shunned in church, Hatrack retires on Sunday night to the graveyards, where she practices her trade. Devout to the end, she takes her Catholic customers to the Protestant cemetery, and vice versa. She is paid according to their whims—Midwestern men are miserly, especially in matters of vice—and consequently expects little.

---

[45]Singleton, *H. L. Mencken and the* American Mercury *Adventure,* 52–53, 56–58.

When a customer offers her a dollar, she concludes the story by remarking ingenuously that she has no change.[46] This innocuous piece is hardly, by any reasonable standards, worthy of censorship. Asbury offers no graphic description of sexual activity. Nor does he titillate his readers, for he draws Hatrack as a physically unattractive, indeed almost pathetic, figure. In addition, Asbury offers no moral affirmation of his protagonist. Hatrack is no magnanimous Jennie Gerhardt, for whom honor is a matter of fidelity rather than virginity, no woman of character such as Tess Durbeyfield, who is destroyed by the irreconcilable conflict between religion and the natural law. Although Asbury does indict moral hypocrisy, he says nothing that had not already been said before, and more scathingly. Yet the Reverend J. Franklin Chase, a Methodist preacher and the secretary of the Boston Watch and Ward Society, found the essay "immoral" and "full of filthy and degrading descriptions." Chase also believed that "a whole high-school class of unwedded mothers may be the result of a lascivious book." Between 1918 and 1926, he and the Watch and Ward Society suppressed between fifty and seventy-five books in Boston.[47]

---

[46]Herbert Asbury, "Hatrack," *American Mercury* 7 (April 1926): 479–83. The "Hatrack" affair has been discussed at length by Mencken and a variety of critics. Mencken offers the fullest account in the eight volumes of the "The Hatrack Case, 1926–1927" (EPFL) Mencken's narrative has been published, without his annotations, in *The Editor, The Bluenose and the Prostitute: H. L. Mencken's History of the "Hatrack" Censorship Case*, ed. Carl Bode (Boulder, CO: Roberts, Rinehart, 1988) 37–174. Also, see Edgar Kemler, *The Irreverent Mr. Mencken* (Boston: Little, Brown, 1950); 191–216; Manchester, *Disturber of the Peace*, 187–207; Singleton, *H. L. Mencken and the* American Mercury *Adventure*, 167–81; Bode, *Mencken*; Fred Hobson, *Mencken: A Life* (New York: Random House, 1994) 266–69; Hays, *Let Freedom Ring*, 157–92; and Jason Duberman, "H. L. Mencken and the Wowsers," *American Book Collector* 7 (May 1986): 3–14.

[47]Chase's judgment of "Hatrack" is quoted by Kemler, *The Irreverent Mr. Mencken*, 193. Chase's remark about the effect of obscenity is quoted by Manchester, *Disturber of the Peace*, 201. The efforts of the Watch and Ward Society are discussed by Duberman, "H. L. Mencken and the Wowsers," 4.

The line of battle—the iconoclast versus the preacher, the civil libertarian versus the censor—could hardly have been more clear. Drawing upon the hypocrite in Charles Dickens's *Martin Chuzzlewit*, Mencken called Chase a "Pecksniff."[48] Like Sherman during the previous decade, Chase saw Mencken as a destructive element in the United States. Significantly, "Hatrack" was not the first publication in the *Mercury* to generate the society's ire. Mencken had used the September 1925 issue to run "Keeping the Puritans Pure," and the December issue had carried "Boston Twilight," a scathing attack upon the city's culture.[49] When "Hatrack" appeared, Chase seized the chance to challenge his nemesis. On March 30, a vendor in Harvard Square sold the April issue to one of Chase's agents and was arrested. Mencken might well have wished that Chase had chosen a piece of greater merit, but, as he had done previously with *The "Genius,"* Mencken refused to ignore the attack upon freedom of speech. He reasoned that "if Chase were permitted to get away with this minor assault he would be encouraged to plan worse ones, and, what is more, other wowsers elsewhere would imitate him."[50] Mencken decided to force a confrontation and thereby placed himself at considerable risk. If he were found guilty of publishing obscenity, he could face two years in jail.

On April 5, Mencken carried several copies of the *Mercury* to the Brimstone Corner of Boston Common where, centuries before, Puritans had reportedly cast hot brimstone as a reminder to the faithful about the fires of hell. Mencken refused to sell the magazine to one of Chase's assistants. Chase finally appeared and bought the offending issue with a fifty-cent piece. Mencken bit the coin, was arrested, and joined the parade to police headquarters—the short, thick man striding along with his hat

---

[48]Manchester, *Disturber of the Peace*, 188.
[49]See Duberman, "H. L. Mencken and the Wowsers," 6.
[50]Mencken, "The Hatrack Case," 12, EPFL. Quoted by Duberman, "H. L. Mencken and the Wowsers," 8.

pulled low, gesturing with his cigar in his left hand and swiveling his head to take in the spectacle that he had created.[51]

Mencken was tried on April 6 and acquitted the following day. Ebullient, he attacked Chase and proceeded to a lunch at the Harvard Union, where a crowd of more than one thousand met him with cheers. Mencken explained that he had traveled to Boston "to force the censors to abandon back-alley assassinations" and contended that the moralists could be chased out of Massachusetts, just as they had been vanquished in Maryland.[52] Mencken's exuberance was short-lived. In thinking that his victory was final, Mencken badly underestimated his opponent's resourcefulness.

Chase succeeded in having the April issue barred from the mail. This time, Mencken was not even offered the opportunity to defend his magazine. "We wondered why action had been taken without a hearing," Arthur Garfield Hays later wrote scathingly. "Quack medicines and fraudulent stock advertisements are accorded this privilege. Murderous cancer cures circulate, sometimes for months, before they are barred from the mails. But then, they are not obscene—merely fatal."[53] The *Mercury*'s May issue, containing Bernard DeVoto's "Sex and the Co-ed," had already gone to the printer. If this May issue were also banned, then the magazine would lose its second-class mailing privilege, a disastrous situation. At a cost of $8,000, Mencken substituted a piece on learning to play the cello.[54]

In the end, the "Hatrack" affair proved costly in several ways. The *Mercury* lost $20,000 in cash as well as substantial advertising revenue. For the first time, with either the *Smart Set* or the *American Mercury*, the guardians of public virtue forced Mencken to withdraw a piece that he had accepted for publication.

---

[51]Singleton, *H. L. Mencken and the* American Mercury *Adventure,* 172.

[52]Kemler, *The Irreverent Mr. Mencken,* 205.

[53]Hays, *Let Freedom Ring,* 180. Quoted by Duberman, *H. L. Mencken and the Wowsers,* 12.

[54]Singleton, *H. L. Mencken and the* American Mercury *Adventure,* 179.

Despite overwhelming evidence to the contrary, Mencken's detractors insisted that the whole episode in Boston was nothing but a cheap publicity stunt.[55] Mencken was shocked, and then dismayed, that his fellow journalists did not offer stronger support. Many failed to see that his cause was theirs, and everybody's.

On the other hand, Mencken took a bold stand for freedom of speech, the cause that he valued above all others. During the battle, Mencken once more proved an exhausting opponent. Just as William Jennings Bryan had died soon after the Scopes trial, Chase died in November 1926. Echoing what he said after Bryan's departure, Mencken said of Chase: "We killed him."[56] Perhaps they did, but it was only the individual who died, not the cause. In denouncing censorship, Mencken was attacking one of the most deeply ingrained Puritan traditions in American life. In 1929, the port of Philadelphia banned the writing of Rabelais. Later, when the tumult was over, Mencken chose to caricature Chase as a fool who "amuses me magnificently."[57] Chase's beliefs, though, generated no amusement, and Mencken likely came to suspect that censorship was a disease that would never be eradicated in America. Although its germs might lie dormant for a while, this plague would inevitably return, and while other timorous souls capitulated and crept away, it would remain for Mencken and other bold individuals like him to take their stand for freedom of speech.

The *Mercury's* circulation continued to increase during 1926; by the end of 1927 it reached 80,000 and peaked at about 84,000 in early 1928.[58] This marked the magazine's zenith under Mencken's editorship. In his forty-eighth year, Mencken had succeeded, certainly beyond his own expectations, with the journal established to console and entertain America's civilized minority.

---

[55]Ibid., 177–78.

[56]Kemler, *The Irreverent Mr. Mencken*, 214.

[57]Mencken to Cornelia McQueen Gibbs, 20 March [1930], in Bode, *The New Mencken Letters*, 243.

[58]Singleton, *H. L. Mencken and the* American Mercury *Adventure*, 156.

The *Mercury* had an appreciable influence upon other periodicals, and Mencken became America's most influential magazine editor.[59] Although a number of his competitors offered more money, Mencken's magazine, as George Douglas has remarked, maintained consistently higher standards than any other American periodical up to this time.[60] Significantly, the passage of time has accentuated Mencken's achievement. While many magazines date quickly—they seem archaic after a decade, to say nothing of well more than half a century—a journey through the *Mercury*'s first five years is never boring.

By this point in the 1920s, Mencken had become, in the words of biographer Carl Bode, "a national institution."[61] His success with the *Mercury* was complemented by his eminence as a journalist and continued productivity as a philologist. Through his newspaper copy in Dayton and his courage in Boston, he had established himself as a national spokesperson for First Amendment rights. Even those who despised Mencken acknowledged his stature. Michael Gold, for example, later spoke sardonically of "King Mencken."[62] Few men of letters have achieved such prominence in America. Mencken's reign, however, could not last indefinitely. Just as a number of matters effected Mencken's ascent, several issues contributed to his decline.

As a social critic, Mencken was victimized by his own proficiency. While the Depression hastened the *Mercury*'s decline, it did not initiate it. As the circulation figures show, the magazine's popularity had begun to ebb more than a year and a half before the stock market crash of 1929. The response to the *Prejudices* series showed a similar decline in the public's interest.

---

[59]Bode, *Mencken*, 207, 241. See Bode, *Mencken*, 258–62; and Singleton, *H. L. Mencken and the* American Mercury *Adventure*, 181–87.

[60]George Douglas, *H. L. Mencken: Critic of American Life* (Hamden, CT: Archon Books, 1978) 32.

[61]Bode, *Mencken*, 242.

[62]Michael Gold, "At King Mencken's Court," in *The Hollow Men* (New York: International Publishers, 1941) 11–25.

The series stopped in 1927, after the publication of the sixth volume as well as a *Selected Prejudices*. He had written so insistently, and with such success, that there was less real need for his social commentary.

The year before the *Prejudices* series ended, Mencken failed to help his reputation with *Notes on Democracy*, the first volume of a trilogy completed during the 1930s with *Treatise on the Gods* and *Treatise on Right and Wrong*. Although Mencken did respect three theoretical elements of democracy—equality before the law, limitation of government, and freedom of speech—he found "all the rest of the democratic dogma...at best dubious and at worst palpable nonsense."[63] He believed that democracy, like Puritanism, was founded upon the envy of inferior people for their betters, that democracy appealed to the weaklings in the battle of life, not to those self-reliant individuals who boldly made their own way. Refusing to believe in the equality of intelligence or ability, Mencken deplored what he saw as the leveling process under democracy, whereby a culture was reduced to its lowest common denominator. Repeatedly borrowing Nietzsche's image of the herd, the Baltimorean laughingly employed a number of other animal analogies—oxen and swine, for example, and goats and donkeys—to ridicule the common citizen. Since he thought that the ordinary citizen could not vote intelligently, Mencken rejected universal suffrage. He concluded that "democracy, in the last analysis, is only a sort of dream. It should be put in the same category as Arcadia, Santa Claus, and Heaven."[64] Given the importance of this subject for Mencken, and given the controversial nature of his ideas, *Notes on Democracy* could have been one of his most accomplished and provocative books. Unfortunately, it proved considerably less.

The aforementioned epistolary debate with the wealthy socialist Robert Rives La Monte had caused Mencken to scoff at

---

[63]Mencken, *Minority Report: The Notebooks of H. L. Mencken*, 119–20.
[64]Ibid., 278.

democracy, and he began making notes for this volume around 1910.[65] Mencken began his manuscript around 1923, but the writing did not proceed smoothly. Moreover, he was interrupted by his coverage of the Scopes trial and the uproar over "Hatrack" the following spring. Mencken finally completed *Notes on Democracy* in June 1926, and the volume shows the author's strain.[66]

This study of 212 pages, appreciably shorter than the other two volumes of the trilogy, falls into four sections of unequal length, all marked by Mencken's irony. "Democracy came into the Western World," Mencken caustically begins in "Democratic Man," his first section, "to the tune of sweet, soft music. There was, at the start, no harsh bawling from below; there was only a dulcet twittering from above. Democratic man thus began as an ideal being, full of ineffable virtues and romantic wrongs—in brief, as Rousseau's noble savage in smock and jerkin, brought out of the tropical wilds to shame the lords and masters of the civilized lands." Classicist and patrician, Mencken snorts at the notion that among the lower classes there "lies a deep, illimitable reservoir of righteousness and wisdom, unpolluted by the corruption of privilege." Mencken proceeds to explain the conflict between democracy and the natural law and the degree to which democracy, like its counterparts theology and superstition, addresses itself to emotion rather than reason. Mencken complains that, for the mindless democratic man, "Greek...is only a jargon spoken by bootblacks, and Wagner is a retired baseball player."[67] Unlike Walt Whitman, Mencken shuddered at the democratic vistas.

The second section, "The Democratic State," discusses the difference between representational government and direct

[65]Mencken, "Professor Veblen," in *Prejudices: First Series* (New York: Knopf, 1919) 60.

[66]Adler, *The Mencken Bibliography*, 12.

[67]Mencken, *Notes on Democracy* (New York: Knopf, 1926) 3, 4, 60.

democracy and explains the problems caused by disproportional representation and lame-duck officials. In a democracy, Mencken remarks sardonically, elected officials must truckle to the mob: "The bargaining is conducted to the tune of affecting rhetoric, with music by the choir, but it is as simple and sordid at bottom as the sale of a mule.... It is a combat between jackals and jackasses." If these politicians are donkeys, then they are also whores, "men who have sold their honor for their jobs."[68] In a democracy, as Mencken depicts it, one cannot be both an honorable individual and a politician.

Shorter than their predecessors, the book's final sections, "Democracy and Liberty" and "Coda," unnecessarily hurry *Notes on Democracy* to its conclusion. Mencken explains that democracy, more than any other form of government, inevitably conflicts with common decency. He laments the inability of Americans to be happy, their refusal to trust one another and coexist peacefully in a civilized society. Concerned in his "Coda" with the future of democracy, Mencken returns to the doctrine of the insoluble and speaks scornfully of democracy as a bogus panacea for inequalities generated by the natural law. After bemoaning again the lack of intellectual aristocracy in America, Mencken turns from his subject with laughter rather than with ire. While he cannot respect democracy intellectually, he does find it "the most charming form of government ever devised by man." The ringmaster applauds democracy as "a show of the first cut and calibre. Try to imagine anything more heroically absurd. What grotesque false pretenses! What a parade of obvious imbecilities."[69] And what a shame that Mencken did not make more of his material and hence write a better book.

Although Mencken's iconoclasm and his ability as a stylist make *Notes on Democracy* entertaining, he had said much of this before, and just as proficiently. Moreover, the book's informal title

---

[68]Ibid., 98, 177.
[69]Ibid., 206, 208

announces its casual structure, for these notes contain needless repetition. Here as elsewhere, Mencken writes more successfully as a satirist than as a political scientist. He sees the French Revolution as an abject failure and Karl Marx as "a philosopher out of the gutter."[70] When *Notes on Democracy* is compared to a book such as *To the Finland Station*, Edmund Wilson's immensely readable history of socialism, Mencken's faults as an historian are patent: too much fulmination and too little reasoned analysis, too great a reliance upon the glittering phrase and too little attention to solid research. Financially, *Notes on Democracy* was not successful. Although the book did receive some praise, Mencken acknowledged later that most of the reviews were decidedly unfriendly. Always honest about his writing, Mencken came to see *Notes on Democracy* as his worst book.[71] It tended to lessen Mencken's credibility among his more educated readers.

Likewise, some of Mencken's conclusions about literature hurt his reputation, as did his failure to recognize books of undeniable merit. During the previous decade, Mencken had immersed himself in literature; this saturation, for the most part, generated sound judgments and reviews of high quality. During all of 1926, on the other hand, Mencken reviewed only twenty-four novels in the *American Mercury*; he also devoted one article to poetry. This amount of material would have been covered during a productive three months on the *Smart Set*. Not surprisingly, Mencken's acuity as a critic declined along with his interest in literature and his familiarity with it. It was especially unfortunate that Mencken shifted his attention elsewhere during the 1920s, for these ten years and the 1850s mark the two most fertile decades in American literary history. Some of the books that Mencken now ignored proved far more significant than a number of volumes on which he had lavished so much attention previously. For example,

---

[70]Ibid., 7.
[71]Adler, *The Mencken Bibliography*, 12. Mencken to Norman Foerster, 28 October 1933, in Bode, *The New Mencken Letters*, 206.

Mencken neglected to review *The Sun Also Rises* (1926) as well as Thomas Wolfe's *Look Homeward, Angel* and William Faulkner's *The Sound and the Fury*, both published three years later. This is in no sense a blanket condemnation of Mencken's literary criticism during the 1920s. As both editor and critic, he continued to do an immense amount of good for both neophytes and established writers. Mencken strongly influenced Sinclair Lewis, the first American to win the Nobel Prize for literature. Mencken had published Lewis in the *Smart Set* in 1916, when he was still a minor author; moreover, Mencken gave Lewis the idea underlying *Babbitt* (1922), the novelist's acid portrait of the American businessman. Lewis in turn dedicated *Elmer Gantry* to Mencken and, in the Nobel Prize address delivered in Stockholm, praised the Baltimorean's contributions to American literature. With his insistent satire of the American scene, Lewis was the novelist of the 1920s whose perspective Mencken most appreciated. Just as Mencken had used Dreiser's writing earlier to attack the censors, he employed Lewis's novels as a point of departure to burlesque the *booboisie*.

Praising *Main Street* (1920), Mencken said just as much about his own view of America as about the novel's artistic merit. Mencken called Lewis's protagonists, Carol Milford Kennikott and her husband, Will, "triumphs of the national normalcy—she with her vague stirrings, her unintelligible yearnings, her clumsy gropings, and he with his magnificent obtuseness, his childish belief in meaningless phrases.... Here is the essential tragedy of American life, and if not the tragedy, then at least the sardonic farce."[72] And here as well was Mencken's own portrait of the *boobus Americanus*, that creature of banal aspirations and inflated self-importance. Mencken found *Babbitt* superior to *Main Street* and, in a review revealingly entitled "Portrait of an American Citizen," said that he had known George Babbitt for nearly three

[72]Mencken, "Consolation–I–an American Novel," *Smart Set* 64 (January 1921): 138–40.

decades. Examine the protagonist, Mencken urged his readers, "and you will know what is wrong with the land we live in." Mencken called his review of *Elmer Gantry*, Lewis's scathing portrait of a preacher, "Man of God: American Style." Finding this novel more laudable than either *Main Street* or *Babbitt*, Mencken said that Gantry expounded the "immemorial bilge of his order." Lewis's colleagues, Mencken explained, "spend themselves upon riddles of personality. He depicts a civilization."[73] While he was justified in praising Lewis's skill as a satirist, Mencken was very wrong about some of the novelist's colleagues, who most certainly did not squander their considerable talents by depicting mere personality. Rather, they detailed, with great force and sweep, what was past and passing in America and speculated, with little optimism, about what was to come.

The year before *Elmer Gantry* appeared, Scribner's had published a slim volume about a Midwestern dreamer, courting wealth and approval, who meets a violent death among the ash heaps in New York. As a youngster, Jay Gatsby serves an apprenticeship under Dan Cody, a figure with clear ties to the golden age of the American West. Naively underestimating the importance of social class in America, Gatsby believes that he can actually win his golden girl. Even after losing Daisy Fay to a mindless brute with money and an Ivy League education, Gatsby continues to insist, all evidence to the contrary notwithstanding, that he can recapture the past. *The Great Gatsby* details the American dream gone sour: illusions that end with a corpse in the swimming pool in the fall with America's vitality, reduced to a thin circle of blood, spiraling down the drain; with a funeral, for a man's life and a country's aspirations, to which nobody comes; and with a house, once brightly lit and pulsing to the serenades of

---

[73]Mencken, "Portrait of an American Citizen," *Smart Set* 69 (October 1922): 138–40. Mencken, "Man of God: American Style," *American* Mercury 10 (April 1927): 506–8. See Stephen A. Young, "The Mencken-Lewis Connection," *Menckeniana* 94 (Summer 1985): 10–16.

money and music and laughter, now gone dark. Only that "final guest who had been away at the ends of the earth," Fitzgerald comments through his narrator, Nick Carraway, near the end of the novel, "didn't know that the party was over."[74] Carried by the haunting lyricism of Fitzgerald's prose, *Gatsby* offers a dirge for America.

At the end of 1925, Boni and Liveright had released the story of Clyde Griffiths, Theodore Dreiser's exhaustive saga of American life. With a sympathy for Clyde that never degenerates into sentimentality, *An American Tragedy* chronicles the uneven struggle between ignorance and poverty on the one hand and wealth, privilege, and power on the other. The son of a pathetic itinerant preacher, Clyde dreams incessantly—about more money and better clothes, about a more prestigious job and a prettier girl—in that shadowy world of illusion that characterizes the American experience. Overcome by desire and knowing nothing about contraception, Clyde impregnates Roberta Alden, a young factory worker, and then is drawn irresistibly to Sondra Finchley, another rich golden girl who exploits him as part of her tawdry rebellion against parental authority. After Roberta's death, Clyde, like a frightened animal, is hunted down mercilessly by the law and then executed. Clearly indicating Dreiser's ability to shape this large mass of material, the ironic metaphor appearing in chapter 1 expands into symbol and functions throughout the novel as a structural device. From "The Door of Hope, Bethel Independent Mission" in Saint Louis, the adolescent proceeds inevitably to that final, horrible door marking the execution chamber in New York State, figuratively the place of retribution for all victims, all vain dreamers, such as Clyde.[75] The "Souvenir" concluding the novel marks its highly effective circular structure. Russell, the illegitimate son of Clyde's sister who has been

---

[74] F. Scott Fitzgerald, *The Great Gatsby* (New York: Scribner's, 1953) 182.
[75] Theodore Dreiser, *An American Tragedy* (New York: New American Library, 1964) 13.

abandoned by a traveling man, replaces his executed uncle in the family hierarchy. Dreiser's implication is chilling: Clyde's demise cannot teach anybody anything, and poor Russell awaits the same fate. *An American Tragedy* "seemed to me," Dreiser explained to a correspondent, "to include every phase of our national life.... It seemed so surely a story of what life does to the individual—and how impotent the individual is against such forces."[76] Far more than a mere depiction of current civilization, the novel encompasses the national experience and sets forth the American dream, the indigenous national myth, gone awry.

Just as *The Great Gatsby* was Fitzgerald's most accomplished novel up to this time, so was *An American Tragedy* Dreiser's. (These novels would ultimately rank as the greatest achievements in each writer's canon and would subsequently be regarded as two seminal texts in American literary history.) What Sinclair Lewis attempted, he did well, but Fitzgerald and Dreiser did far more. One certainly does not have to denigrate *Tom Sawyer* in order to praise *Huckleberry Finn*, but one must understand that the latter, because of its technical proficiency and scope, is a more significant work of art. One would never know, from Mencken's reviews of *The Great Gatsby* and *An American Tragedy*, that tragedy is a more profound art form than satire.

In May 1925, Mencken's assessment of *The Great Gatsby* appeared on consecutive days in the Baltimore *Evening Sun* and the *Chicago Sunday Tribune*. Mencken applauded Fitzgerald's improvement as a stylist since the publication of *This Side of Paradise* and praised the novelist as a social historian. On the other hand, Mencken called Gatsby a "clown," a protagonist with "the simple sentimentality of a somewhat sclerotic fat woman." Jordan Baker, Fitzgerald's symbol for the new woman—sleek in build, as fast and as deadly as the models of cars providing her

---

[76]Theodore Dreiser to Jack Wilgus, 20 April 1927, in *Letters of Theodore Dreiser: A Selection*, 2 vols., ed. Robert Elias (Philadelphia: University of Pennsylvania Press, 1959) 458.

first and last names—should have interested the author of *In Defense of Women*, but Mencken cavalierly dismissed her as "a crooked lady golfer." Unaccountably, Mencken called the narrator, Nick Carraway, "a symbol of the new America." Honest in the midst of deceit, restrained in the face of garish consumerism, Nick actually stands opposed to the chaos and false values swirling around him. In July, Mencken's review of only 250 words appeared in the *American Mercury*. While he again praised Fitzgerald's improvement as a stylist, Mencken denigrated the novel's plot. He felt obliged to say no more. Neither review, then, gave any indication that Mencken perceived the enormity of Fitzgerald's achievement.[77]

Mencken's review of *An American Tragedy* was longer but no more perceptive. For personal and professional reasons, the Mencken-Dreiser relationship had grown increasingly bumpy during the 1920s. Mencken had burlesqued Dreiser's experimental writing and ridiculed his personal life. Dreiser, in turn, had found Mencken narrow-minded and managerial. In the old days, Mencken had hastened to get his laudatory reviews of Dreiser's books into print. "Dreiser in 840 Pages," however, did not appear in the *Mercury* until two months after *An American Tragedy* was published, a period during which the literary establishment, Stuart Pratt Sherman included, had reversed its position on Dreiser and praised the novel. During its first six months, *An American Tragedy* sold 30,000 copies and earned Dreiser $18,000. The novelist who had struggled so desperately after *Sister Carrie* now incorporated himself for tax purposes.[78] Mencken's denigration of

---

[77]Mencken, "Fitzgerald, the Stylist, Challenges Fitzgerald, the Social Historian," Baltimore *Evening Sun*, 2 May 1925. Mencken, "Scott Fitzgerald and His Work," *Chicago Sunday Tribune*, 3 May 1925. Mencken, "New Fiction," *American Mercury* 5 (July 1925): 382.

[78]Richard Lehan, *Theodore Dreiser: The World of His Novels* (Carbondale IL: Southern Illinois University Press, 1974) 172. W. A. Swanberg, *Dreiser* (New York: Scribner's, 1965) 318.

the novel, a huge financial and critical success, exasperated Dreiser and astonished others.

Reviewing *The Financier* in 1912, Mencken had refused to say that Dreiser's material had overwhelmed him. However, Mencken called *An American Tragedy*, with Dreiser's controlling hand apparent throughout, "a shapeless and forbidding monster." Criticizing Dreiser's style, Mencken held up for ridicule some of the novel's more awkward prose. *An American Tragedy*, however, is written far more proficiently that *Jennie Gerhardt* and *The Titan*, whose style Mencken had applauded the decade before. Mencken also belittled the novel's plot: "A simple tale. Hardly more, in fact, than the plot of a three page story in *True Confessions*." While recounting the novel's series of events, however, Mencken revealed that he had not read the novel attentively. "[Clyde's] reply is to take [Roberta] to a lonely lake and drown her," Mencken summarized, and he later spoke nonchalantly of Roberta's "murder." Actually, the scene is far more problematic—similar to the incident in *Sister Carrie* where Hurstwood is conscience-stricken in front of the safe in the saloon. The safe shuts accidentally; money in hand, Hurstwood can only flee. Is he guilty, then, of robbery? *An American Tragedy* revolves to a similar degree around the events at Big Bittern. Clyde does not push Roberta into the lake; she falls accidentally when bumped by his camera. Certainly, Clyde is guilty of a sin of omission because he refuses to save the downing woman. Is he guilty, though, of murder? The novel clearly posits an ambiguity that Mencken failed to perceive. Later in the review, Mencken praised *An American Tragedy* "as a human document...full of solemn dignity," but he closed with a jibe at Dreiser's supposed moralizing.[79] For the second time in a year, Mencken failed to recognize a landmark publication in American literature.

---

[79]Mencken, "Dreiser in 840 Pages," *American Mercury* 7 (March 1926): 379–81.

Initially, Dreiser was disgusted and sent Mencken a letter so insulting that it halted the correspondence for more than eight years. The novelist, however, grew resigned. Sometime during the spring or summer of 1926, Dreiser encountered Charles Angoff, Mencken's assistant on the *Mercury*. "That boss of yours ought to stay in Baltimore on the *Sun* and keep out of writing about books," Dreiser said. "[Eugene] O'Neill is luckier than the rest of us. He has George Jean Nathan to write about him. Now, Nathan knows playwriting.... But Mencken—oh, well. What does it matter anyway?"[80]

The age of Mencken did not end, however, because he exasperated Dreiser and declined in acuity as a literary critic. It did not end because Mencken neglected to review novels of undeniable merit or wrote a book as patently flawed as *Notes on Democracy*. Nor did it end because Mencken the satirist wrote and edited so proficiently that he helped to make his social criticism obsolete. The most significant cause substantially overshadowed Mencken's errors and self-defeating expertise: America changed, and he chose not to.

In 1922, enthralled by the follies of his native land, Mencken exclaimed that "only the man who was born with a petrified diaphragm can fail to laugh himself to sleep every night, and to awake every morning with all the eager, unflagging expectations of a Sunday-school superintendent touring the Paris peep-shows." But Americans stopped laughing after October 29, 1929—not because of petrified diaphragms but because of a national unemployment that swelled past 25 percent and carried with it horrible mornings of shattered careers, separated families, and long breadlines. Some men jumped off buildings. Others slept out in the cold, wrapped in newspapers and huddled over heating grates. This was a chilling turn for a country begun with such great

---

[80]Dreiser to Mencken, 8 February 1926, in Riggio, *Dreiser-Mencken Letters*, 554. Charles Angoff, *H. L. Mencken: A Portrait from Memory* (New York: Yoseloff, 1956) 101.

expectations. After a long run, Mencken's circus finally closed. During his golden decade, Mencken drew upon the Garden of Eden myth to depict America as "The Paradise of backslappers" and the "Eden of clowns."[81] During the 1930s, a decade of hard times and diminishing dreams, it would remain for Mencken to come to terms with America after its fall from grace.

---

[81]Mencken, "On Being an American," in *Prejudices: Third Series*, 14, 19, 64. Fitzpatrick, *Gerald W. Johnson*, 141.

CHAPTER 5

The Late H. L. Mencken: 1930-1939

> I have been through so many burial ceremonies that I am beginning to feel like a veteran. I'll never believe that I am actually dead until they stuff me beautifully and deposit me in the National Museum at Washington.
>
> −Mencken to Theodore Dreiser, 6 October 1936, in Dreiser-Mencken Letters: The Correspondence of Theodore Dreiser & H. L. Mencken, 1907–1945

While the 1920s marked Mencken's zenith, the 1930s witnessed his nadir. His kingdom vanished as the Depression worsened. By 1932, unemployment reached 13,000,000, and the Bonus Army camped in Washington that summer. The show *Americana* featured the haunting lyrics and lugubrious melody of "Brother, Can You Spare a Dime?" Sometime during the 1930s, Mencken made this sweeping, strident entry in his notebook: "Despite all the current blah about new incentives to industry (Communism), the duty of every man to submerge himself in the state (Fascism), and the wickedness of people who save their money and look out for themselves otherwise (the New Deal), individualism still survives…. [A]ll the really important business of the world must be done by single men, operating under the compulsion of their own egos."[1] Voting records suggest that most Americans strongly disagreed.

Like those dark days before and during World War I, the Depression tested Mencken's resolve. Dissenting again from the current view of things, he spoke loudly and at length for the adversary culture in his native land. In brief, he despised what he viewed as America's pathetic slide into the welfare state. In this decade of grand causes and noble sentiments, years marked by lofty talk of brotherhood and solidarity, Mencken the individualist still urged his readers to think for themselves. As a civil libertarian, he defended the right of the American Communists to be heard, but he saw them as nothing more than wayward children laughable in their gullibility. Seizing the opportunity provided by the signing of the Nazi-Soviet Pact in August 1939, Mencken sardonically entitled a newspaper column "Triumph of Idealism." "It is hard not to laugh at the current situation of the American pinks," he snorted, "those excessively hopeful and confiding boys and girls. In the short span of a single calendar week they have tobogganed precipitously from the topmost pinnacles of the Rock Candy Mountain to the nether depths of the Slough of Despond."[2] During this decade of belief, Mencken continued to endorse skepticism. "[T]here is always," he had remarked years earlier in a famous aphorism, "an easy solution to every human problem—neat, plausible, and wrong."[3] He found no reason to change his mind. Utopia does not exist, he argued repeatedly, and he scoffed at spurious messiahs and their heated devotees: "all the dubs and misfits of the world [who dream] of New Jerusalems."[4]

[1]Mencken, *Minority Report: H. L. Mencken's Notebooks* (New York: Knopf, 1956) 207–208.

[2]Mencken, "Triumph of Idealism," Baltimore *Evening Sun*, 25 August 1939.

[3]Mencken, "The Divine Afflatus," in *A Mencken Chrestomathy* (New York: Knopf, 1949) 443.

[4]Mencken, "The Pathology of Radicalism," Baltimore *Evening Sun*, 13 April 1936.

During a decade marked by considerable guilt on the part of bourgeois intellectuals who turned on the class that had nourished them, Mencken refused to beat his breast and chant *mea culpa*. In his view, feeling guilty had become a national pastime; for him, this emotion was as sterile as it was misguided. In these years marked by the growth of proletarian literature—writers believing that their fiction could improve the world and critics demanding that artists ally themselves with the working class—Mencken continued to believe that the true artist does the most good by writing well. Art is not a handbill, Mencken insisted. He chastised John Steinbeck for writing "pink hooey" in *The Grapes of Wrath* and dubbed the radical writers "illuminators of the abyss." "Good literature is never concocted by students of political mountebanks," Mencken explained characteristically; "it is the work of men to whom all politicians, of whatever school, are only comic characters with red noses in baggy pants."[5] Once again, Mencken laughed at matters that some others took very seriously. As so much change swirled about him in politics and literature, Mencken remained, as Theodore Dreiser explained it, "just a realist contemplating things realistically."[6]

Mencken's attitudes during the 1930s and the response to them raise questions central to an understanding not only of his career but also of the American experience during the twentieth century. Had the engaging ringmaster of the previous decade quickly degenerated into a walking anachronism? Was Mencken nothing more than an aging performer playing inappropriate material to a hostile audience that rudely emptied the theater as he

---

[5]Mencken to H. L. Davis, 17 May 1939, in *Letters of H. L. Mencken*, ed. Guy J. Forgue (New York: Knopf, 1961) 436. Mencken, "Illuminators of the Abyss," *Saturday Review of Literature* 11 (6 October 1934): 155–56. Mencken, "The Arts," *Cosmopolitan*, 98 (January 1935): 24.

[6]Theodore Dreiser to Mencken, 4 October 1936, in *Dreiser-Mencken Letters: The Correspondence of Theodore Dreiser and H. L. Mencken, 1907–1945*, 2 volumes, ed. Thomas P. Riggio (Philadelphia: University of Pennsylvania Press) 611.

tottered about the stage? Or was he, instead, the most eloquent of America's conservative critics during a decade of needless upheaval?[7] Did the 1930s offer Mencken the invaluable opportunity to resume his role as pioneer, a pathfinder who struggled to lead America out of the maze of radical rhetoric? Was his refusal to change not unenlightened stubbornness but rather an unwavering devotion to common sense—a case of Mencken's ability to keep his head while so many of those around him were losing theirs? Paradoxically, these years of Mencken's fall from favor prove some of the more intriguing ones for posterity. He suspected correctly that America's response to the Depression would mark a watershed in the nation's history.

Mencken the private citizen differed dramatically from the public figure. The man who gave away his overcoat to that transient in Times Square and acknowledged to a colleague in Baltimore that "you can't have people starving on your doorstep" refused, as a writer, to view the Depression in apocalyptic terms.[8] He saw it as no earthquake, no warning about the essential wrongness of things under capitalism. In Mencken's eyes, bust followed boom as a matter of course. If left alone, the economy would right itself, just as it had done after the bad times in 1893 and 1894.

Throughout the decade, Mencken used a medical metaphor to explain his position. "All that can be said of a certainty," he wrote in 1932, "is that the patient is very far from dead, and that the chances seem to be very good that he will recover eventually.... He is howling for more medicine. Well, let him howl himself out. He will fall asleep soon or late, and wake up feeling better."[9] Accepting the validity of an old medical adage, "First, do no harm," Mencken endorsed *vis medicatrix naturae* (nature's

---

[7]See Carl Bode, *Mencken* (Carbondale IL: Southern Illinois University Press, 1969). 307-313. See W. H. A. Williams, *H. L. Mencken* (Boston: Hall, 1977) 144, 147.

[8]Bode, *Mencken*, 294.

[9]Mencken, "The Present Discontent," Baltimore *Evening Sun*, 6 June 1932.

remedy). But the great majority of Americans wanted something with a more impressive label, something that promised quicker results. After they found it, Mencken ridiculed "the anatomy of quackery" and "Dr. Roosevelt."[10] Only two years apart in age, Mencken and the President were worlds apart in background and perspective. Mencken's battle with FDR marked the most important conflict in the Baltimorean's career, a battle that lasted longer, exhibited more acrimony, and had far higher stakes than his previous combat with Wilson, Bryan, and Chase.

Disgusted with the continuation of Prohibition during Herbert Hoover's presidency, Mencken voted for FDR in 1932. Obviously, Mencken could not foresee the sweeping changes that would mark Roosevelt's first "Hundred Days." Beginning in the spring of 1933 and continuing up until American entered World War II, Mencken attacked Roosevelt in every available forum. During the presidential campaign of 1936, Mencken supported, and subsequently befriended, Governor Alf Landon of Kansas, the Republican candidate who carried only two states. The next year, Mencken blasted Roosevelt's unsuccessful effort to pack the Supreme Court. Mencken criticized what he viewed as Roosevelt's lack of respect for the Constitution, the Brain Trust's efforts to curb freedom of speech, and the President's use of the futile hopes of forlorn people to further his own lust for power. At times, Mencken spoke as the humorist of old: he likened the New Deal to Christian Science and called the Social Security Act "a fantastic burlesque of a law."[11] On other occasions, he plotted inventive assaults. In 1938, for example, while he was editing the *Evening Sun*, Mencken published "Object Lesson," six columns filled with one million dots, one for each federal jobholder. He

---

[10]Mencken, "The Anatomy of Quackery," Baltimore *Evening Sun*, 16 December 1935. Mencken, "Three Years of Dr. Roosevelt," *American Mercury* 37 (March 1936): 257–65.

[11]Mencken, "A Planned Economy," Baltimore *Evening Sun*, 5 February 1934; and "Wizards at Work," Baltimore *Evening Sun*, 9 September 1935.

thereby graphically depicted the scope of the federal dole.[12] On the other hand, Mencken grew increasingly exasperated, and sometimes downright disgusted, as the decade passed. He resorted, as he had never done earlier, to the heavy tones of the jeremiad and predicted doom for his native land. In 1935, borrowing again from Defoe, Mencken proposed to Alfred A. Knopf a book with the bludgeoning title of *Diary of a Plague Year*; it was never published. Bemoaning the seeming disappearance of the law of supply and demand, Mencken spoke repeatedly about the futility of robbing Peter to pay Paul. Insisting that every bill no matter how adeptly postponed, must ultimately fall due and be settled, Mencken filled his newspaper columns with financial imagery: "Balance Sheet," "Something for Nothing," and "Paying the Piper: It Will Be a Sad Day When the New Deal Bills Fall Due."[13]

Mencken also took a larger accounting, and his dispute with Roosevelt far transcended the issue of deficit spending. This conflict between the President and his articulate, persistent gadfly involved contrary conceptions of the American experience. For Mencken, the underdog in the United States was not one of life's victims but rather that individual who acquired competence at a trade, paid the bills, refused to holler for help during bad times, and otherwise served as a respectable citizen.[14] Mencken never doubted that, once the mentality of the dole was established, continued expectations of public assistance would erode the American work ethic. Believing strongly in self-reliance, Mencken

---

[12]Mencken "Object Lesson," Baltimore *Evening Sun*, 10 February 1938.

[13]Mencken, "Balance Sheet," Baltimore *Evening Sun*, 12 April 1937; "Something for Nothing," Baltimore *Evening Sun*, 5 June 1933; and "Paying the Piper: It Will be a Sad Day When the New Deal Bills Fall Due," New York *American*, 17 December 1934.

[14]Mencken was decidedly influenced in these views by William Graham Sumner's concept of the "forgotten man." See Douglas C. Stenerson, "The 'Forgotten Man' of H. L. Mencken," *American Quarterly* 18 (Winter 1966): 686–96. Also, see Williams, *H. L. Mencken*, 118–122; George Douglas, *H. L. Mencken: Critic of American Life* (Hamden, CT: Archon Books, 1978) 153; and Bode, *Mencken*, 250–52.

concluded that the New Deal robbed people of their self-respect; he called it "a complete repudiation of the traditional American moral system."[15] Coincidentally, Mencken began his career as a professional writer the year in which Horatio Alger died. In brief, Mencken in his fifties found no reason to change the conclusions reached decades before in *The Philosophy of Friedrich Nietzsche*. The strong person's gain necessarily marks the weak person's loss. To destroy the threat of failure is also to destroy incentive. With his fundamental pessimism, Mencken viewed the New Deal as an abomination. He shook his head and responded to Roosevelt as he responded to all visionaries before or since. Your efforts to improve the scheme of things are futile, was always the gist of Mencken's rejoinder. Divide the wealth; deal the cards anew, again and again. But you will find, if you let the game naturally run its course, that the intelligent person will play proficiently and leave the table with more money than was brought, and that the incompetent player will be a chronic loser. You may mean well, but you are misguided and dangerous. Your efforts to restructure American society are doomed because you cannot change the nature of humankind.

Whatever its logic, Mencken's position was costly. Mencken found his financial imagery turned upon him, for it was he, not President Roosevelt, who paid the piper. Some of the attacks upon Mencken verged upon hysteria, but he had been bludgeoned before, and the vituperation meant little to him. He had never, however, received outright dismissal as an intellectual force. In July 1935, the Cleveland *Press* spoke of "the late H. L. Mencken."[16]

Among the forums in which he wrote, Mencken suffered least as a journalist. Mencken had long been a local institution, and his "Monday Articles" ran until early 1938, when they ceased during

---

[15]Mencken, "Utopia Eat Utopia," Baltimore *Evening Sun*, 20 August 1934.
[16]Elrick B. Davis, Cleveland *Press*, 20 July 1935. Quoted by Bode, *Mencken*, 313.

his stint as editor of the *Evening Sun*. In May of that year, he began a Sunday column that ran into the next decade. During 1934 and 1935, Mencken also wrote a weekly column for the New York *American*, material that was picked up by several other Hearst papers.[17]

Although he remained very much in public view as a newspaperman, Mencken's reputation as a magazine editor declined precipitously. The Depression that imperiled many American magazines—the *Smart Set*, for example, folded in 1930—exacerbated the previous decline in circulation of the *American Mercury*. This was hardly surprising, given the editorial policy that Mencken set forth in the magazine's first issue and then followed vigilantly. Calling the *Mercury* "entirely devoid of messianic passions," Mencken asserted that "the Editors have heard no Voice from the burning bush. They will not cry up for sale any sovereign balm...for all the sorrows of the world.... The world, as they see it, is down with at least a score of painful diseases, all of them chronic and incurable."[18] While such insouciance was attractive during a balmier decade, Mencken's flippancy seemed archaic, if not downright offensive, during a time when, for millions of Americans, "the sorrows of the world" meant something far more than a glib phrase on a piece of paper. Nathan stopped contributing to the magazine in 1930—he and Mencken were feuding, although neither would acknowledge it publicly—and the Baltimorean chose not to write an editorial about the Depression until 1932. The *Mercury*'s circulation fell from 62,000 in 1930 to about 30,000 in 1933. Mencken resigned

---

[17]Betty Adler, *H. L. M.: The Mencken Bibliography* (Baltimore: Johns Hopkins University Press, 1961) 114–116.

[18] "Editorial," *American Mercury* 1 (January 1924): 27. This unsigned editorial is written in the third-person plural, but the ideas, the diction, and the cadences of the prose clearly identify the writing as Mencken's.

as editor with the December 1933 issue, and Alfred A. Knopf sold the magazine the next year for only $25,000.[19] Ever stoical, Mencken rationalized his resignation in his parting editorial as well as in his correspondence. Ten years with any magazine was long enough—his editorship of the *Smart Set* had also lasted about a decade—and, after reviewing more than 4,000 volumes, he concluded that he had done more than his share for "the swell letters of his native land." Moreover, he looked forward to having more time to devote to his books.[20] Whatever Mencken's reasons, his critics seized the chance to celebrate his departure. When he left the *Mercury*, Mencken lost the most significant national forum he had heretofore possessed, and he would never again acquire a comparable one.

An ancillary event, the founding of the *American Spectator* in 1932, hardly brightened Mencken's mood or made him more sanguine about human nature. This unbound, four-page monthly, in no sense an imposing publication, was edited by Ernest Boyd (the Irish literary critic who had written a book about Mencken in 1925), Nathan, Dreiser, James Branch Cabell (whose *Jurgen* Mencken had defended against the censors), and Eugene O'Neill. Even Herbert Asbury, whose "Hatrack" Mencken had defended at considerable personal risk, contributed to the new magazine. The *American Spectator*'s first issue ran an editorial that, although it did not name Mencken or the *Mercury*, implicitly disparaged both.[21] The next issue carried Dreiser's "The Great American Novel," a harsh, lengthy, and sometimes inaccurate commentary upon Mencken's faults as a literary critic. Stoical once again,

---

[19]For a detailed discussion of the magazine's decline during the 1930s, see M. K. Singleton, *H. L. Mencken and the* American Mercury *Adventure* (Durham, NC: Duke University Press, 1962) 215–41.

[20]Mencken, "Ten Years," *American Mercury* 30 (December 1933): 385–87. Mencken to J. B. Dudek, 21 October 1933, in *The New Mencken Letters*, ed. Carl Bode (New York: Dial Press, 1977) 295–96. Mencken to A. G. Keller, 4 October 1933, in Forgue, *The Letters of H. L. Mencken*, 367–68.

[21]Singleton, *H. L. Mencken and the* American Mercury *Adventure*, 227/49.

Mencken said that the *American Spectator* was not to be taken seriously and would not last long. He was correct, at least on the second count, for the magazine, marked by a good deal of editorial squabbling and turnover, folded in 1937.[22] The facts remain, though, that a number of Mencken's colleagues, some of whom he had helped appreciably during better days, established a competitor to Mencken's foundering magazine and, in Dreiser's case, denigrated him by name. Mencken had to rely, once again, upon the resources of his individualism.

As an author of books, Mencken experienced a greater mix of success and failure than he did as a magazine editor. Less productive than he had been during the 1920s, he published four volumes that covered theology, politics, morality, and philology. Some sold far beyond his most optimistic expectations; others were virtually ignored. While some critics extolled Mencken, others vilified him or dismissed him altogether. Once more, Mencken reacted demonstrably to neither triumph nor disaster.

Treatise on the Gods, the second volume of the trilogy begun four years before with *Notes on Democracy*, appeared in March 1930. This third-generation agnostic avoids the proselytizing of the believer as well as the self-righteous invective of the person who denounces religion after initially embracing it. More often than not, Mencken's perspective is, as he claims, one of "amiable skepticism." Mencken laughs at the "subtle flattery" of the collector for the missions: "It is his function to warm his victims into charity toward their inferiors."[23] The Baltimorean likens the saga of Jesus Christ to "the sempiternal Cinderella story, lifted to cosmic dimensions." The common man, Mencken explains, embraces religion not out of reverence but rather out of fear and gullibility. Mencken predicts no end to the market that allows

---

[22]Dreiser, "The Great American Novel," *American Spectator* 1 (December 1932): 1–2. Mencken disparaged the magazine in letters to Raymond Pearl, 29 January 1933 (Princeton University) and to Philip Goodman, 23 February 1933 (Princeton University).
[23]Mencken, *Treatise on the Gods* (New York: Knopf, 1930) v, 67.

theologians to hawk their wares so successfully. Clearly, *Treatise on the Gods* offers Mencken a showcase for his considerable talent as an ironist. In this substantial study of more than 350 pages, Mencken succeeds, as he had done in the first three editions of *The American Language* but as he had failed to do with the *Nietzsche*, in making a complex subject accessible to a popular audience. The layman who studies religion, Mencken explains in his preface, "quickly finds himself lost in an impenetrable jungle," and it remains for the author, serving again as a pioneer, "to open a few paths."[24]

"The Nature and Origin of Religion," the first of the book's five chapters, immediately reveals Mencken's irreverence. Religion in America, remarks the opponent of censorship and Prohibition, "is used as a club and a cloak by both politicians and moralists, all of them lusting for power and not a few of them palpable frauds."[25] This chapter proceeds to discuss the myth of the Great Flood, the early calamities that spawned gods and priests, and the ways in which these priests dealt with challenges to their authority. The second chapter, "Its Evolution," explains that religion has grown more complicated as the number of gods has increased. Mencken discusses the similarities between pagan and Christian myth and, citing Spain as an example, remarks that various religions have tried to usurp power from the state. The third chapter, "Its Varieties," argues that similarities among religions outnumber the differences, discusses several rituals with their totems and taboos, and sets forth various theories about life after death. Detailing the ways in which various religions conceive of their creator, Mencken remarks sportively that some have viewed God as a muskrat and a beaver.

The book's longest chapter, "Its Christian Form," sketches the history of this church and speaks of the textual problems in both the Old and New Testaments. Mencken discusses the Higher

---

[24]Ibid., 347, v.
[25]Ibid., 1.

Criticism (the study of the Bible as a literary text rather than as divine revelation) and praises the Authorized King James translation as "probably the most beautiful piece of writing in all the literature of the world." Revealing his own convictions, Mencken speaks of the ways in which Jesus's teaching have been misinterpreted: "The egalitarianism that He preached was anything but the political egalitarianism that we know today, and it is thus absurd to call Him, as many do, the father of Socialism." The volume's final chapter, "Its State Today," becomes even more polemical as Mencken argues with those who extol the virtues of religion: "If the theological answer to all questions had ever actually prevailed in the world the actual progress of the race would come to an end.... Everything that we are we owe to Satan and his bootleg apples." Mencken stresses an old theme, what he sees as the irreconcilable conflict between science and religion, and details the conflict between religion and freedom of thought. After noting the antipathy among various religions, Mencken remarks, with characteristic irony, that "every religion of any consequence, indeed, teaches that all the rest are insane, immoral and against God. Usually it is not hard to prove it."[26]

Treatise on the Gods finally proves both a work of scholarship and a platform that allows Mencken to perform as he pleases: to turn his skepticism and pungent style upon beliefs that millions of Americans hold dear, to indict the cruelty with which supposedly religious people deal with one another, and to laugh unrestrainedly about the ways of God to man. Mencken viewed this provocative, highly readable synthesis as his best book. Predictably, *Treatise* generated huge controversy; moreover, it sold well. When the book appeared in early 1930, the Depression had not yet taken its full hold on the American economy, and the book market had not declined as much as it would later. The book went through seven printings and sold more than 13,000 copies its

---

[26]Ibid., 243, 261, 315, 343.

first year.[27] In the end, this subject that Mencken wrote about with "amiable skepticism" treated him most kindly. His next two books did not.

Making a President, ironically subtitled *A Footnote to the Saga of Democracy*, appeared two years later. In this scissors-and-paste job completed in thirty-six hours, Mencken collected his writings concerning the 1932 presidential conventions in Chicago: dispatches that had run in the *Sunpapers* and some editorials from the *American Mercury*.[28] While the book's preface provides a fascinating insider's view of convention coverage, there was little market, during this worst year of the Depression, for a volume that essentially offered yesterday's news.[29] *Making a President* sold only 1,520 copies during 1932; the book's ephemeral nature became even more evident the following year, when the public purchased only twenty-one copies. H. Allen Smith, the book editor for the United Press who wrote favorably about Mencken on other occasions, advised his readers that they would have more fun by taking thirty rides on a streetcar than by spending $1.50 for the Baltimorean's political commentary.[30]

Treatise on Right and Wrong was published in 1934. This study of more than 300 pages, which Mencken calls a "sort of companion volume" to *Treatise on the Gods*, uses the same five-

---

[27]Mencken called *Treatise on the Gods* his best book in "Autobiographical Notes, 1941," EPFL. For the book's sales and publication history, see Adler, *The Mencken Bibliography*, 15. For the controversy generated by the book, see Sara Mayfield, *The Constant Circle: H. L. Mencken and His Friends* (New York: Delacorte, 1968) 152–53. For a very illuminating analysis of Mencken's attitude toward religion, see Charles A. Fecher, *Mencken: A Study of His Thought* (New York: Knopf, 1978) 81–148. For a thorough discussion of the book's composition, see Mary Miller Vass and James L. W. West III, "The Composition and Revision of Mencken's *Treatise on the Gods*," *Papers of the Bibliographical Society of America* 77 (Fourth Quarter 1983): 477–61, reprinted under the same title in *Menckeniana* 88 (Winter 1983): 9–16.

[28]Manchester, *Disturber of the Peace*, 259–60.

[29]For a discussion of the book's preface, see Bode, *Mencken*, 314–17.

[30]Quoted by Manchester, *Disturber of the Peace*, 260.

chapter format as its predecessor. In a style generally lacking Mencken's characteristic vitality, *Treatise on Right and Wrong* covers some very old ground: the conflicts between faith and reason, determinism and free will, and romanticism and classicism, as well as the differences between Hellenism and Hebraism and the Reformation and the Renaissance. Given its moment in American history, *Treatise on Right and Wrong* seems less interesting for Mencken's scholarship on the history of morality—his strengths clearly lay elsewhere—than for his own quest for order in time present. How is the contemplative, civilized individual to survive, Mencken wonders repeatedly, in a world where the established footholds are rapidly disappearing? Denouncing the believer's "slavish and preposterous surrender of will," Mencken again exhorts his readers to shun all saviors, be they religious or political, and to take responsibility for their own lives. Praising Aristotle, Mencken sets forth his own credo: "He was all for temperance, moderation, reasonableness. The ideal world that he envisioned was not peopled by angels, nor even by philosophers, but by healthy, decent, intelligent, fair-minded, honorable men."[31] Highly impressionistic, *Treatise on Right and Wrong* stands, in its Byzantine way, as Mencken's *De Profundis*, his plea for sanity and decorum in a world gone mad.

Always perceptive and honest about his own writing, Mencken knew that *Treatise on Right and Wrong* was flawed. While the book was written under difficult circumstances, his wife's declining health and his own departure from the *Mercury*, Mencken characteristically made no excuses. After the volume was published, he told a correspondent that "I'll never write another book like [it.] The materials I collected were so enormous that I was lost in them several times and had to be rescued by police radio cars. At the end I heaved overboard at least twenty pound of notes. My fear is that the book shows this strain. Maybe

---

[31]Mencken, *Treatise on Right and Wrong* (New York: Knopf, 1934) v, 222, 198.

I'll go back to it in a few years and try to smooth things out a bit."[32] Although *Treatise on Right and Wrong* sold nearly 3,000 copies during the first half of 1934, sales declined to fewer than 500 during the rest of the year and to only 80 copies during the first half of 1935. Sensibly, Mencken resisted the urge to revise the book. Instead, he turned again to his philology, a happier and far more rewarding subject.

In 1936, thirteen years after the appearance of the third edition, Alfred A. Knopf published the fourth edition of *The American Language*. This edition differs from its predecessors not only in its structure but also in Mencken's conclusions about the relationship between British and American English. While Mencken had previously used the image of "diverging streams" to depict their differences, he asserts here that, because of the increasing dominance of American English, the dialects are now actually converging.[33] This fourth edition received much critical acclaim and sold better than any of Mencken's previous books. The volume made the best-seller list for non-fiction, and the Book of the Month Club, offering *The American Language* as a dividend to its subscribers, took an additional 90,000 copies. The reception of this fourth edition marked, in Charles Fecher's phrase, "the beginning of [Mencken's] critical rehabilitation."[34]

In April of that year, the same month that *The American Language* appeared, the *New Yorker* further enhanced Mencken's rehabilitation by publishing "Ordeal of a Philosopher." This marked the first appearance of the autobiographical sketches later collected in the *Days* books. Mencken offers here no more jeremiads about Roosevelt's America. Instead, the congenial

---

[32]Mencken to Harry Leon Wilson, 29 October 1934, in Forgue, *Letters*, 379–80.

[33]Mencken, *The American Language* (Fourth Edition) (New York: Knopf, 1936) vi. See Fecher, *Mencken: A Study of His Thought*, 299–300. See also Williams, *H. L. Mencken*, 223.

[34]Fecher, *Mencken: A Study of His Thought*, 296. For further discussion of the book's reception, see Mayfield, *The Constant Circle*, 223.

raconteur casts his eye back upon a better day. He gleefully recounts the antics of Old Wesley, a colorful figure who, at the end of the nineteenth century, lived in the alley behind Hollins Street. Although some adults were skeptical about Old Wesley, the youngsters had the good sense to love him. Ever scornful of metaphysicians, Mencken has Wesley define truth as "something that only damned fools deny." Mencken reminisces that Old Wesley, after being upbraided by a clergyman for living in sin, "always won the ensuring bout in moral theology, for he had packed away in his head a complete roster of all the eminent Biblical characters who had taken headers through No. 7."[35] Delighted, the *New Yorker* called for more material; another piece appeared in 1937, and nine more ran in 1939.[36]

With these autobiographical narratives, Mencken discovered an art form conducive to his abilities as a storyteller (one of the more patently Southern aspects of his character), as a comic writer, and as a winsome social historian. As he acknowledged, these dramatic sketches with relatively little dialogue were hardly short stories.[37] Moreover, his handling of the subject was not mimetic; he called the sketches "buffoonery" and, echoing *Huckleberry Finn*, admitted to a few "stretchers" along the line.[38] Thinking it impossible for the author to tell the truth about his own life, Mencken looked out rather than in and thereby avoided the error of talking too much about himself.[39] He discovered a wealth

---

[35]Mencken, "Ordeal of a Philosopher," *New Yorker* 12 (11 April 1936): 21–24. This appeared in *Happy* Days under the title "The Career of a Philosopher."

[36]Adler, *The Mencken Bibliography*, 154–56.

[37]Mencken to Mrs. K. S. White of the *New Yorker*, 9 January 1936. Quoted by Brother James Atwell, F. S. C. (Brothers of the Christian Schools) "Eclipse and Emergence," *Menckeniana* 24 (Winter 1967): 4.

[38]Mencken to Louis Untermeyer, 16 January 1943, in Bode, *Letters*, 512. Mencken, *Happy Days: 1880–1965* (New York: Knopf, 1940) vi. The frequency and scope of these "stretchers" are proven by the material in "Additions, Corrections, and Explanatory Notes" to the *Days* Books, EPFL.

[39]Mencken, *Minority Report,* 241.

of material that he found relatively painless to write. The success
of these sketches genuinely surprised him; they came too easily,
he thought, to be considered so good. In his middle-to-late fifties,
Mencken showed an adaptability that belied his years. His sojourn
in the American desert was over.

Like a number of other writers, Mencken pondered the
relationship between life and art. He began his most difficult
decade by enumerating, in *Treatise on the Gods*, the deities who
have captivated humankind and subsequently disappeared.
Mencken could hardly have anticipated the fury of his future
assaults upon those whom he would excoriate as false messiahs.
He finished *Treatise on the Gods* on Thanksgiving night, 1929,
about one month after the stock-market crash. He could not then
foresee that, in the coming decade, there would be many fewer
opportunities for American to give thanks, or that he would
experience the death of a spouse, declining health, and a profound
fall from favor. Containing some of Mencken's more cogent
prose, the book's conclusion exalts skepticism and stresses
humankind's need for a "proud imperturbability." Mencken lived
what he wrote, and he endured once more. "The brethren who
have been celebrating my funeral," Mencken informed a
correspondent in 1935, "may have a surprise in store for them."[40]
By the end of the decade, after transcending personal tragedy,
witnessing the success of *The American Language*, and playing to
high acclaim the role of American elegist, Mencken could
justifiably assert that the reports of his death had been
exaggerated.

---

[40]Mencken, *Treatise on the Gods*, 352. Mencken to JimTully, 28 September
1935, in Forgue, *Letters*, 395.

CHAPTER 6

Wink at a Homely Girl: 1940-1956

We live in a land of abounding quackeries, and if we do not learn to laugh we succumb to the melancholy disease which afflicts the race of viewers-with-alarm. I have had too good a time of it in this world to go down that chute.

–*Mencken, preface to* A Mencken Chrestomathy

The combination of triumph and disaster that marked the 1930s extended, albeit in a different way, into the years from 1940 to 1956, a period split by Mencken's debilitating stroke on November 23, 1948. Taking much pride in the productivity of his seventh decade, Mencken published six books between 1940 and 1948: the *Days* trilogy; *A New Dictionary of Quotations*, a long-standing project that finally appeared in 1942; and two supplements to *The American Language*, issued in 1945 and 1948. To posterity's benefit, the nine years prior to the stroke were distinguished, more than any previous period in Mencken's career, by the coalescence of time future, present, and past.

With his penchant for order and ever mindful of posterity, Mencken set his lands in order. He made final the disposition of his literary estate and worked hard to complete several detailed, candid records for future scholars. In addition to continuing the diary begun in 1930, Mencken devoted four volumes to "My Life as Author and Editor" and three to "Thirty-Five Years of

Newspaper Work." Out of deference to those still living, he placed this material under time-lock, to be released at intervals of fifteen, twenty-five, and thirty-five years after his death.[1] He showed no such restraint in discussing current events. Continuing to view the New Deal as an abject failure, Mencken believed that Roosevelt planned to rush American into World War II to resuscitate the economy. He predicted that Roosevelt would lose the election of 1940 if America had not entered the war by that time. Ever the Anglophobe, Mencken thought that England would use America for its own self-interest and argued, as he had before America entered World War I, that this country's professed neutrality was bogus.[2] He again found himself differing with the *Sunpapers*. "It seems silly," he informed a correspondent in January 1941, "to go on trying to tell the truth in a paper that has swung so far toward Roosevelt."[3] While he remained on salary as a consultant, Mencken stopped writing for the newspaper the next month and did not resume until 1948.

---

[1]See Bode, *Mencken* (Carbondale IL: Southern Illinois University Press, 1969) 285–86; and Sara Mayfield, *The Constant Circle: H. L. Mencken and His Friends* (New York: Delacorte Press, 1968) 285–86. Mencken made sizable bequests to the Enoch Pratt Free Library, the New York Public Library, and Dartmouth University. In 1971, a substantial collection of correspondence at the New York Public Library became accessible to scholars. In 1981, the "Diary" became accessible to scholars, as did Mencken's three-volume commentary on the autobiographical trilogy and the four-volume "Letters and Documents Relating to the Baltimore *Sunpapers*." "My Life as Author and Editor" and "Thirty-Five Years of Newspaper Work" became accessible to scholars in 1991. See the afterword to this volume, where I discuss the lively response to the publication of some of this material.

[2]Mencken to Theodore Dreiser, 11 April 1939, 6 September 1939, and 2 October 1939, in *Dreiser-Mencken Letters: The Correspondence of Theodore Dreiser and H. L. Mencken, 1907–1945*, 2 volumes, ed. Thomas P. Riggio (Philadelphia: University of Pennsylvania Press) 639–40, 649, 651. Mencken, "Sham Battle," Baltimore *Sun*, 1 October 1939.

[3]Mencken to Harry Elmer Barnes, 22 January 1941, in *Letters of H. L. Mencken*, ed. Guy J. Forgue (New York: Knopf, 1961) 453.

However, he found other forums in which to discuss the contemporary scene. In 1946, *Life* magazine conducted an interview during which Mencken blasted the United Nations and the National Labor Relations Board. Despite Roosevelt's death the previous year, Mencken spoke no more optimistically about life in his native land: "The world is a shambles. The country is a wreck. Truman is as transparent a fraud as Roosevelt ever was, and far more of a fool." American politics, Mencken remarked pointedly, is incompatible with honesty and common sense.[4]

Two years later, Mencken traveled with an interviewer, Donald H. Kirkley of the *Sunpapers*, for a recording session at the Library of Congress. In this voice made husky by a cold and marked by a pronounced Baltimore accent—residents of this fair city live in "Bawlamer," in the state of "Merlin"—one hears the marvelous cadences of Mencken's prose, the living American tongue that so delighted him. He disparaged idealism and higher education and laughed at the imbecility of those who write letters to the editor as well as the tastes of Americans in general. Once again, he scoffed at politicians: "In politics, I am a complete neutral. I think they're all scoundrels." However, Kirkley was also concerned, wisely so, with something besides Mencken's caustic response to current events. Under Kirkley's prodding, Mencken briefly surveyed, from the height of his sixty-eight years, some of the events marking his long and turbulent career: the early newspaper days, "The Free Lance" and its attendant controversy, and the experiences on the *Smart Set* and the *American Mercury*.[5]

While Mencken found the present unpalatable and the future uncertain (but most probably worse than the present), he found the past attractive. Finally, it was Mencken the raconteur rather than the journalist, the American elegist rather than the strident critic of the contemporary scene, who found pronounced success during

---

[4]Roger Butterfield, "Mr. Mencken Sounds Off," *Life* 21 (5 August 1946): 45–46, 48, 51–52.

[5]*H. L. Mencken Speaks*, Caedmon Records (TC-1082).

the 1940s. The *Days* books, whose sixty chapters allowed the leisurely recollections that a recorded interview could not, stand as one of Mencken's greatest achievements, a moving paean to an age that, in his eyes, merits nostalgia. These volumes showcase one of American letters' most distinguished stylists. He writes so superbly that he ranks as a writer of prose nonfiction with Benjamin Franklin and Henry David Thoreau, Mark Twain and Henry Adams—lofty company indeed.

"We were lucky to have been born so soon," Mencken asserts characteristically in the collected edition of the *Days* books. Mixing irony with regret, he proceeds to explain what America has lost but what his art can capture and hence preserve:

> As the shadows close in we can at least recall that there was a time when people could spend weeks, months, and even years without being badgered, bilked, or alarmed.... The human race had not yet succumbed to the political and other scoundrels who have been undertaking of late to save it, to its infinite cost and degradation. It had a better time in the days when I was a boy, and also in the days when I was a young newspaper reporter, and some of that better time even slopped over into the first half of the space between the two World Wars. I enjoyed myself immensely, and all I try to do here is to convey some of my joy to the nobility and gentry of this once great and happy Republic, now only a dismal burlesque of its former self.[6]

Mencken's conclusion here is hardly unique. In this lament for a once-remarkable country that has lost its way, he resembles earlier American elegists such as F. Scott Fitzgerald at the conclusion of *The Great Gatsby* and John Dos Passos in "Vag," the compelling coda to the *USA* trilogy. But while the *Days* books mourn a

---

[6]Mencken, author's note, in *The Days of H. L. Mencken: Happy Days, Newspaper Days, and Heathen Days* (New York: Knopf, 1947) vi.

vanished America, they also vibrantly celebrate a more colorful, less homogeneous age. Mencken's trilogy offers a remembrance of things past from the perspective of an American bourgeois who abhors romanticism, practices the plain style, delights in the bizarre and indelicate, and takes full advantage of the continued appeal, perhaps more mythic than factual, of the good old days. The combination is salubrious.

Covering 1880 to 1892, birth to puberty, *Happy Days* stands as Mencken's "Fern Hill." "An aging man's memory," he remarks, "searches through his lost youth for bursts of complete felicity." During those days of innocence, boys misbehaved by hooking rides on horse trucks, stealing sweet potatoes and roasting them on the sly, sneaking cigarettes and reading dime novels. They watched the circus parade and fed ice cream to Frank, the family pony, when he stuck his head through the dining-room window. The children loved the neighborhood hostler and affectionately regarded the police as comic figures. Mencken gratefully recalls elementary school during "those days when psychiatrists still confined themselves to running madhouses." He laughs at his sojourn in Sunday school—he was sent not to be converted but rather because his father wanted to nap undisturbed on Sunday afternoon—and delights in the alley evangelists and their colorful churches: "the Watch Your Step Baptist Temple, the Sweet Violet Church of God, [and] the Ananias Pentecostal Tabernacle." *Happy Days* concludes with Mencken's response to his grandfather's death: "For a brief instant, I suppose, I mourned my grandfather, but...a vagrom and wicked thought ran through my head. I recognized its enormity instantly, but simply could not throttle it. The day was a Thursday—and they'd certainly not bury the old man until Sunday. No school tomorrow!"[7]

---

[7] Mencken, *Happy Days: 1880-1892* (New York: Knopf, 1940) 113–14, 21, 183, 312–13.

Happy Days appeared in January 1940. With war in Europe and America hardly happy under the continuing pall of the Depression, Mencken's book perhaps appealed to many readers less as autobiography than as a welcome pastoral tale. *Happy Days* sold over 9,500 copies during the first six months—it made the best-seller list by April—and received some lavish praise. It has been said that this book contains the most accomplished prose written in America since Mark Twain's death in 1910. Mencken himself reread *Huckleberry Finn* every year and perhaps smiled to himself when he found *Happy Days* described as "thoroughly delightful recollections...seasoned with the buoyant wisdom of advancing age. A book to be read twice a year by young and old alike, as long as life lasts."[8]

Published in 1941, *Newspaper Days* covers 1899 to 1906, the period from Mencken's first appearance in the Baltimore *Herald* until his move to the Baltimore *Sun*. With the characters populating this memoir—a superintendent of the morgue and a prison warden, press agents and judges, bartenders and policemen, restaurant owners and newspaper editors—Mencken leaves a cache of Americana. He gleefully devotes the chapter entitled "Slaves of Beauty" to newspaper artists, one of whom, after being fired, agrees to paint a biblical backdrop for one of the "evangelical filling stations" in the South: those concrete tanks, some with the luxury of hot water, that offer baptism by total immersion. "The result," Mencken recollects laughingly, "was most probably the most splendiferous work of ecclesiastical art since the days of Michelangelo.... The Tower of Babel was made so high that it bled out of the top of the painting...and from a very Red Sea in the foreground was thrust the maw of Jonah's whale, with Jonah himself shinning out to join Moses and the children of

---

[8]Russell Blankenship compares Mencken's prose to Mark Twain's in *American Literature as an Expression of the National Mind* (New York: Cooper Square Publishers, 1973) 763. The passage quoted is by Edmund Weeks, "The *Atlantic* Bookshelf," *Atlantic Monthly* 165 (March 1940): unnumbered page.

Israel on the beach."[9] The painting proved a huge success among the hordes concerned less with verisimilitude than with piety. Unable to take religion seriously, Mencken again reduces belief to burlesque. Mixing instruction with delight, Mencken recounts several tales where the wages of sin are far from death. In "The Days of the Giants," he marvels at the gargantuan appetites of the time. One elderly gentleman of means, past hearing the call of the flesh, takes pleasure in the same dinner every evening for years. He begins with three whiskeys and proceeds to two double porterhouse steaks and double helpings of several vegetables, all washed down by two quarts of wine. Dinner ends with three more whiskeys and a cigar. Gluttony and intemperance play no part in his demise; rather, he dies of pneumonia after being hit by a bicycle.

In "A Girl from Red Lion, Pa.," a widely anthologized sketch, Mencken offers the uplifting tale of a farm girl seduced by her beau, Elmer. Convinced by religion that she is damned to lead a life of sin, she takes the train to Baltimore in search of work in a brothel. Greeted at the station by an agent of salvation named Peebles, an honest hack driver who refuses "to take more than three or four times the legal fare from drunks," she is driven to the sumptuous establishment of Miss Nellie d'Alembert, a madame with the proverbial heart of gold. A visiting newspaperman, who remembers his *Huck Finn*, preaches the sermon: "I advise you to go home, make some plausible excuse to your pa for lighting out, and resume your care of his cows. At the proper opportunity take your beau to the pastor, and join him in indissoluble love. It is the safe, respectable, and hygienic course. Everyone agrees that it is moral, even moralists."[10] With the blessing of all present, the young woman returns to Red Lion and, the reader surmises, an honorable Elmer. The Hollywood censors, Mencken remarks mischievously at the end of the tale, veto several attempts to make this

---

[9]Mencken, *Newspaper Days: 1899–1906* (New York: Knopf, 1941) 171.
[10]Ibid., 228, 236.

saga into a movie script. As he had done decades before in "Puritanism as a Literary Force," Mencken decries the perverse effects of moral convention. The humor carrying these sketches, however, has replaced the violent assault marking the essay. The wise clown, Mencken turns the world of conventional virtue upside down. In Mencken's case, as in so many others', youth was mostly wasted on the young. The grandeur of his "salad days as a journalist," he ruefully came to recognize, could be perceived only in retrospect. During this "Golden Age," the young managing editor was addressed as "Colonel Mencken." A good dinner cost sixty cents, and beer ran twelve mugs to the keg. For the most part, the American citizen was left alone. "That pestilence of Service...was just getting under way," Mencken remembers warmly, "and many of the multifarious duties now carried out by...the vast rabble of inspectors, smellers, spies and bogus experts of a hundred different faculties either fell to the police or were not discharged at all."[11] An older man recalling a younger century, Mencken told the poet Edgar Lee Masters that "we were passing through Utopia, and didn't know it."[12] *Newspaper Days*, Mencken's rollicking version of Utopia, sold over 6,000 copies during its first few months.

Heathen Days, the trilogy's final volume, was published in 1943. Having covered his youth and young adulthood, Mencken's memoirs were drawing closer to time present. Not wanting to embarrass the living, Mencken chose to backtrack here and offer "a series of random reminiscences" stretching from 1890 to 1936."[13] Traversing America, Mencken recalls the hangings that he covered as a young reporter, the garish events of the Scopes trial (in a chapter portentously called "Inquisition"), and the

---

[11]Ibid., 215, 200, 205.

[12]William Manchester, *Disturber of the Peace: The Life of H. L. Mencken* (New York: Harper, 1950) 293.

[13]Carl Bode, *Mencken* (Carbondale IL: Southern Illinois University Press, 1969) 258. Mencken, *Heathen Days: 1890–1936* (New York: Knopf, 1943) vii.

mellow bourbon served at the 1920 Democratic Convention in San Francisco. Unlike its predecessors, *Heathen Days* ventures abroad. Mencken laughs about the YMCA built with American money outside Jerusalem—Moslems come to run on the track—and the tourist shops in Bethlehem that offer souvenirs made in Japan. Mencken's characters in this volume are just as regaling as those filling its predecessors: a gluttonous press agent named A. Toxen Worm; a passenger on an ocean liner, nicknamed the Walrus, who eats 45,000 calories a day; and a high-school mathematics instructor who, much to the delight of his students, goes insane. Establishing his tone in the book's first chapter, Mencken bemoans the demise of Hoggie Unglebower, self-taught veterinarian, rat hunter, and horse trainer, "a magnificent specimen of Natural Man, somehow surviving unscathed every corruption of an effete and pusillanimous civilization." But nothing so good can last. Having fallen in love, Hoggie takes to wearing celluloid collars, overpowering cologne, and huge yellow shoes with pointed toes. As his title suggests, Mencken's perspective as a heathen links these sketches that lack their predecessors' chronological unity. His cogent mix of skepticism and laughter—he calls philosophy "a purely imaginary quantity, like demivirginity or one glass of beer"—enlivens the volume.[14]

As Mencken glances back in this trilogy, he expresses no regrets, a conclusion reached elsewhere during these years prior to the stroke. He declares that "I have had a fine time of it in this vale of sorrow, and no call to envy any man."[15] Eminently comfortable with the forum of the *Days* books, with the latitude to frolic as he pleases—to create and embellish, shock and sigh—Mencken laughs at the follies of his native land and the absurdity of the human predicament. Many Americans are fools of the worst sort, he concludes repeatedly, and much of the eccentricity, and hence the vitality, has disappeared from the national scene. But he urges

---

[14]Mencken, *Heathen Days*, 6, 42.
[15]Ibid., vii.

his readers not to take any of this, or themselves for that matter, too seriously. As much as anything else that he wrote, the *Days* books exhibit Mencken's gusto, his fierce joy, in life itself. Despite his protestations to the contrary, there is a moral here, a famous one expressed millennia before by Epicurus and echoed many times by subsequent writers: *Dum vivimus vivamus* (let us live while we are alive). As the shadows were engulfing America, Mencken also understood that his own days of creativity were numbered.

The next year, Mencken again returned to time past, to his days as city editor early in the century, for *Christmas Story*, a piece that had first appeared in the *New Yorker* and was then reissued by Alfred A. Knopf in 1946 as a small book with illustrations.[16] Mencken recounts here the efforts of Fred Ammermeyer, a Baltimore police lieutenant and infidel who keeps order at the free Christmas dinner that various merchants provide for transients. Disgusted because these transients must endure sermons before they eat, Fred sets out to prove that "philanthropy was by no means a monopoly of gospel sharks." He arranges a dinner open only to "men completely lost to human decency, in whose favor nothing whatsoever could be said." Fred provides a meal with multiple courses, unlimited beer, continuous entertainment, decent cigars, and "complete freedom from evangelical harassment." Satiated, some of the derelicts begin to sing. Old habits die hard, and they launch into "Are You Ready for the Judgment Day?" Then "a quavering, boozy, sclerotic voice" preaches a sermon about salvation.[17]

Like the chapters in the *Days* books, *Christmas Story* shows Mencken's facility with the narrative form and his ability to regale and admonish concurrently. Again, he returns to an old subject: the Puritanical nature of the American sensibility, the extent to

---

[16]The sketch first appeared as "Stare Decisis" [To Stay with Precedent], *New Yorker* 20 (30 December 1944): 17–21.

[17]Mencken, *Christmas Story* (New York: Knopf, 1946): 14, 20, 12, 30.

which virtually very issue or occasion degenerates, despite the best efforts of humane and enlightened people, into a moral matter. Early in 1947, Mencken's Canadian publisher withdrew *Christmas Story* because it was considered sacrilegious.[18] Surely, Mencken was not surprised.

"That Was New York," another robust memoir where Mencken looked back in laughter upon events that had previously made him rage, appeared in the *New Yorker* in 1948. Concerned with the ambiance of life in Greenwich Village during the century's second decade and Theodore Dreiser's presence there, Mencken scoffed at the menagerie of self-proclaimed *artistes*: inept painters, inarticulate writers, and hangers-on of various sorts. Poking fun at their "art-and-love warrens," Mencken explained that "the typical Village menage was made up of a Cubist painter who aspired to do covers for pulp magazines and a corn-fed gal who labored at an erotic novel and paid the bills." Attracted to Dreiser because of his reputation as a maverick and his purported connections with publishers and art dealers, these incompetents pursued him relentlessly with bad manuscripts and worse paintings. More than thirty years before, Mencken and Dreiser had quarreled bitterly over the novelist's insistence upon acquiring, for *The "Genius" Protest*, the signatures of various radicals. Now, with Dreiser dead and the novel largely forgotten, Mencken chose to chuckle: "The nascent Communists of the time were all there, so were the poetical advocates of free love.... Not a few of the handpainted-oil-painted signatories were being pursued by the indignant mothers of runaway daughters."[19] Far past anger over such things, Mencken in his sixty-eighth year delighted in the ridiculousness of it all. His prose had lost none of its vitality, and his skill as a humorist had never been more pronounced. Unfortunately, the time for laughter was growing short. Moreover,

---

[18]Mayfield, *The Constant Circle*, 264.
[19]Mencken, "That Was New York," *New Yorker* 24 (17 April 1948): 53–57.

the final subject that Mencken addressed merited contempt rather than humor.

Mencken returned to the *Sunpapers* in June 1948 and covered the three presidential conventions in Philadelphia: The Republicans that month and the Democrats and the Progressive Party the next.[20] Beginning in August, he wrote sixteen columns, mostly political in nature. His final column, which ran on November 9, discussed something far more important than the follies of democracy's electoral system. A group of blacks and whites was arrested for playing tennis together in Baltimore's city-owned Druid Hill Park. Appalled by such bigotry in the Free State, Mencken wrote caustically that "it is high time that all such relics of Ku Kluxery be wiped out in Maryland."[21] Mencken remained a civil libertarian to the end, and it is appropriate that his final column dealt, as much of his writing had previously, with the issue of personal freedom.

Exactly two weeks later, the stroke changed Mencken's life. After he returned home from the hospital, he stubbornly tried to continue on as before. In January 1949, for example, he corresponded with Mrs. Theodore Dreiser. One of America's most distinguished stylists, the author who less than nine months before had written that rollicking satire of Greenwich Village, now wrote a letter with garbled syntax.[22] It reeks of mortality. Although Mencken could no longer write, he remained in public view. Some

---

[20]These columns are reprinted in *Mencken's Last Campaign: H. L. Mencken on the 1948 Election*, ed. Joseph C. Goulden (Washington, DC: New Republic Book Company, 1976).

[21]Mencken, "Equal Rights in Parks: Mencken Calls Tennis Order Silly, Nefarious," Baltimore *Sun*, 9 November 1948. Reprinted under the title "Mencken's Last Stand" in *The Vintage Mencken*, ed. Alistair Cooke (New York: Vintage Books, 1955) 227–30; and under the title "Mencken Calls Tennis Order Silly, Nefarious," in *The Impossible H. L. Mencken: A Selection of His Best Newspaper Stories*, ed. Marion Elizabeth Rodgers (New York: Doubleday, 1991) 204–206.

[22]Mencken to Mrs. Theodore Dreiser, 14 January 1949 (University of Pennsylvania).

old material was reprinted, and some previously unpublished material appeared. Fittingly, it seems, even these final years involved controversy. *A Mencken Chrestomathy*, which he assembled prior to the stroke, was published in June 1949. This collection of more than 600 pages offers an extensive sampling of the writing that had fallen out of print. The volume attests to his range of interests, his grace as a stylist, and his irreverence about nearly everything. "Those who explore the ensuing pages," he warns his readers in the preface, "will find them marked by a certain ribaldry, even when they discuss topics commonly regarded as grave. I do not apologize for this, for life in the Republic has always seemed to be far more comic than serious."[23] This volume gave a new generation of readers far easier access to Mencken's piquant comments on matters such as Woodrow Wilson's saintliness, President Harding's oratory, and William Jennings Bryan's theology. Even in seclusion on Hollins Street, Mencken stirred up the animals once again.

Acknowledgment and misunderstanding marked Mencken's seventieth year. Edgar Kemler's *The Irreverent Mr. Mencken* and William Manchester's *Disturber of the Peace: The Life of H. L. Mencken*, both sympathetic analyses, appeared in 1950. Their publication marked the first book-length studies since the volumes by Boyd and Goldberg and presaged the continuing increase in Mencken scholarship. In May, Mencken was awarded the Gold Medal for Essays and Criticism by the National Institute of Arts and Letters, an unfortunate episode that would not have occurred had Mencken been in full control of affairs. Mencken had a long aversion to accepting awards of any sort and a particular contempt for this organization. In his view, it had opposed freedom of expression in American letters, a cause for which he had fought

---

[23]Mencken, preface, *A Mencken Chrestomathy* (New York: Knopf, 1949) vii. *A Second Mencken Chrestomathy*, edited by Terry Teachout, was published by Alfred A.Knopf in 1995.

long and ardently.[24] Nevertheless, the poet Louis Untermeyer, who had known Mencken for years and hence should have known better, proposed him for the medal in October 1949. Mencken's secretary mistakenly accepted on his behalf, and the announcement was made public. Considerable correspondence ensued, and it was finally decided that the best alternative would be for Mencken to accept the award but miss the ceremony. He could claim poor health as an excuse. Significantly, he did not dictate a statement of acceptance to be read in his absence.[25] This embarrassing episode exacerbated an already difficult time. No matter what a misinformed public must have thought, Mencken remained, as always, outside the literary establishment.

In 1952, Alfred A. Knopf and Mencken's brother August discussed the possibility of issuing a fourth volume of the *Days* books, but the available material proved insufficient.[26] On the other hand, the discovery of Mencken's notebooks made possible the publication, ultimately a posthumous one, of *Minority Report*, a project initiated before the stroke and subsequently interrupted. Mencken approved or vetoed items that his secretary read to him. With its nearly 300 pages, *Minority Report* offers not notes or outlines but rather a combination of aphorisms, paragraphs, and brief essays—in short, the working papers of a professional writer who never lacked material. Most of the items seem to have been composed during the 1930s and early 1940s, and Mencken strikes at a number of long-standing opponents: religion and democracy, Puritanism and pedagogy, Christian Science and the New Deal. As

---

[24]Mencken to Theodore Dreiser, 1 December 1920, 4 January 1935, and 27 March 1944, in Riggio, *Dreiser-Mencken Letters*, 411, 571, 707–708.

[25]See Alfred A. Knopf to August Mencken, 19 April 1950, 24 April 1950, and 28 April 1950; George Jean Nathan to August Mencken, 19 April 1950; August Mencken to Alfred A. Knopf, 21 April 1950; Rosalind Lohrfinck (the secretary of H. L. Mencken) to Douglas Moore (of the National Institute) 24 April 1950; Douglas Moore to August Mencken, 28 April 1950, EPFL.

[26]August Mencken to Alfred A. Knopf, 22 September 1952, 26 September 1952, and 16 October 1952, EPFL.

its title suggests, the book provides the perspective of an adversary culture, in Mencken's view the enlightened minority.[27]

As the shadows lengthened, Mencken's friends took the opportunity to say hail and farewell. In 1953, *The Nation* published "Bouquets for Mencken," a symposium to which William Manchester, James Branch Cabell, Gerald W. Johnson, and nine other contributed.[28] On the occasion of Mencken's seventy-fifth birthday, Alfred A. Knopf published *The Vintage Mencken*, an attractive selection edited by Alistair Cooke, from Mencken's writing in books, magazines, and newspapers. Cooke ended this anthology with the same item that Mencken chose to include in the *Chrestomathy*: his epitaph, which had first appeared in the *Smart Set* in December 1921.

Much had changed since the presidency of Warren Harding. Mencken's reputation had risen, plummeted, and then ascended again. But Mencken, thankfully, found no reason to revise what he had written decades before. He chose not to talk about himself or his writing but rather about people, and he wrote so engagingly that this epitaph would in time become one of his most famous and frequently quoted remarks. The curmudgeon, the polemicist, and the author who wrote so often at the top of his lungs all seemed far away indeed. Instead, in an unusually quiet voice, Mencken acknowledged human imperfection and asked for tolerance: "If, after I depart this vale, you ever remember me and have thought to please my ghost, forgive some sinner and wink your eye at some homely girl."[29] And then he joined Sara in the Loudon Park

---

[27]See Bode, *Mencken*, 374–75.

[28] "Bouquets for Mencken," *The Nation* 177 (12 September 1953): 210–14.

[29]Mencken, "Epitaph," in *A Mencken Chrestomathy*, 627; and in *The Vintage Mencken*, 240. Bode, *Mencken*, 376.

Cemetery in southwest Baltimore, down the road from the old Saint Mary's Industrial School that educated Babe Ruth, another Baltimorean who had enthralled America during a better day.

CHAPTER 7

A Scratch on a Crumbling Stone

There was a man that fought for the right
  And never a friend had he,
'Till after the dawn there dawned the light
  And the world could know and see;
Oh, long was the fight and comfortless,
  But great was the fighter's pride,
And a victor he rose from the storm and stress—
  And after awhile he died

> *Oh, great was the fame but newly found*
> *Of the man that fought alone!*
>   *And the end of it all was a hole in the ground*
>   *And a scratch on a crumbling stone.*

–*Mencken, "Finis," in Mencken,* Ventures into Verse

Shortly after Mencken's death, colleagues at the Baltimore *Sunpapers* opened a locked box containing a note about the handling of his obituary. He had requested only a brief notice, with no accompanying editorial or biographical sketch.[1] He might well have suspected that his request would not be honored. His passing generated numerous retrospectives in Baltimore, throughout America, and abroad. Perhaps the most eloquent was

---

[1]Mencken, note dated 1 June 1943, EPFL.

written by Gerald W. Johnson, the North Carolinian whom Mencken had published in the *American Mercury* and had helped to bring to Baltimore in 1926 to join the staff of the *Sunpapers.* On February 11, 1956, Johnson used the *Saturday Review of Literature* to give thanks for the good times and to celebrate this writer of extraordinary vitality. Mencken "caused a zest for life to be renewed in other men," Johnson remarked in a poignant trope that his old friend would have appreciated; "[he] touched the dull fabric of our days and gave it a silken sheen."[2]

Since that time, as was the case during his career, Mencken has been the subject of numerous attacks—some justified, others unfair. For the most part, though, acclaim has superseded censure. *Menckeniana*, published by the Enoch Pratt Free Library, has appeared quarterly since 1962, and the Mencken Society has flourished since 1976. In 1980, a centennial celebration of considerable proportions was held in several cities. Mencken's house at 1524 Hollins Street, now owned by the city of Baltimore, is a National Historic Landmark. Mencken's books still generate respectable royalties, and he reigns as the most frequently quoted American author.[3] It is one of the more amusing ironies of American literary history—and an irony which Mencken certainly would have relished—that posterity has generally been respectful to one of America's foremost iconoclasts.

Writing in the *New York Review of Books*, Murray Kempton chose an apt image for the Baltimorean's career: Mencken as

---

[2]Gerald W. Johnson, "H. L. Mencken (1880–1956)" *Saturday Review of Literature* 39 (11 February 1956): 12–13. Reprinted under the same title in Johnson's *America-Watching: Perspectives in the Course of an Incredible Century* (Baltimore: Stemmer House, 1979) 199–202; and in *Critical Essays on H. L. Mencken,* ed. Douglas C. Stenerson (Boston: Hall, 1987) 33–37. See the editors' epilogue in *Thirty-Five Years of Newspaper Work: A Memoir by H. L. Mencken,* ed. Fred Hobson, Vincent Fitzpatrick, and Bradford Jacobs (Baltimore: Johns Hopkins University Press, 1994) 374–75.

[3]William Nolte, "The Enduring Mr. Mencken," *Mississippi Quarterly* 32 (Fall 1979): 651–52. Huntington Cairns, "The Quotable Mr. Mencken," *Menckeniana* 54 (Summer 1975): 8–10.

whale, immense and powerful and difficult to capture.[4] For half a century, he played a number of roles and spoke in a wide range of voices. The young reporter and fledgling author developed into an influential literary critic. During the rambunctious 1920s, Mencken cavorted as ringmaster. During the Depression, burlesque gave way to jeremiad. Later, the mellow elegist gratefully celebrated the good times and lamented what American had lost. Because Mencken wrote so prolifically about so many subjects, because he informed and entertained and enraged such a diverse audience, critics have argued bout the type of writing at which Mencken was most proficient and his greatest contribution to American letters. Mencken assessed his career several times. While his conclusions are sometimes debatable—he showed his usual self-deprecation—they provide a sensible point of departure for assessing a career that proved more than a sum of its parts.

Despite Mencken's belief that he would be remembered longest for *The American Language*, journalism always remained his chief interest.[5] He recognized the ephemeral nature of newspaper writing—today's copy, goes an old newspaper joke, wraps tomorrow's fish—but this in no way diminished his enthusiasm. Mencken's coverage of the Scopes trial ranks with his finest writing, and his name merits inclusion in any discussion of the most consequential American journalists. There is a sad irony here, however, that shows how very much we have lost since Mencken's time.

Were Mencken to apply now for a job as a reporter on a major metropolitan daily with the same credentials that he had in 1899, no experience and only a high-school education, he would have little, if any, chance of being hired. Moreover, as columnists on the *Sunpapers* have remarked, a significant portion of

---

[4]Murray Kempton, "Saving a Whale," *New York Review of Books* 28 (11 June 1981): 8, 10–12, 14.

[5]Mencken, "Autobiographical Notes, 1941," EPFL. Mencken, "Henry Louis Mencken," in *Portraits and Self-Portraits*, collected and illustrated by Georges Schreiber (Boston: Houghton Mifflin, 1936) 106.

Mencken's copy might well not be printed today.[6] We are a highly sensitive, very litigious society, and staggering sums can be awarded for an unrestrained sentence, indeed for an intemperate adjective. Mencken might prove too combative and irreverent to be trusted. The qualities that gave Mencken's prose so much vitality are the same features that, in our tamer times, might label him too great a risk. On either count, then, Mencken's lack of academic credentials or his combative copy, journalism today might well spurn the man who graced it for nearly half a century. Such is the result of the proliferation of degrees and America's increased sensitivity.

The man who always spoke favorably of journalism tended, during his later years, to denigrate his efforts as a literary critic. He concluded that criticism "never really interested me profoundly, and such writings of mine as show any promise of surviving lie in other directions." He went so far as to speak of literary criticism as a "vain trade."[7] Despite his casual dismissal of this field and his efforts, Mencken helped to open new possibilities to writers of fiction. Brazen and powerful, he also helped to propagate a critical perspective void of unnecessary deference and a new critical language resplendent with the peculiarly American tongue.

His editing of magazines, Mencken concluded, was only a "sideline" in his career. It was, however, a remarkably productive and influential "sideline." William Manchester has called Mencken "the last of the great cultural editors."[8] Mencken's success is demonstrated less by the *Smart Set*, where he was

---

[6]Matt Seiden, "Do You Think Mencken Would Be Fit to Print Today?" Baltimore *Sun*, 25 June 1984. Gwinn Owens, "Are Some of Mencken's Views Unprintable Today?" Baltimore *Evening Sun*, 1 November 1984. See the editors' introduction in *Thirty-Five Years of Newspaper Work: A Memoir by H. L. Mencken*, xix-xx.

[7]Mencken, "Autobiographical Notes, 1941." Mencken, "Henry Louis Mencken," in *Portraits and Self-Portraits*, 106.

[8]Mencken, "Henry Louis Mencken," in *Portraits and Self-Portraits, 106*. William Manchester, *Disturber of the Peace: The Life of H. L. Mencken* (New York: Harper, 1950) 216.

constantly hamstrung by financial problems and an audience with which he never really felt comfortable, than by the quality of the *American Mercury* during its shining years from 1924 to 1928. The *Mercury* served as the most significant national forum for Mencken's social criticism. Perhaps the greatest testament to Mencken's ability and continuing relevance in this area lies in the frequency with which one hears entreaties similar to the following: "If only Mencken were alive to write about this." The televised spectacle of the Watergate hearings, which he might well have characterized as America's version of bread and circuses, prompted a number of such laments, as has the protracted struggle between evolutions and creationists. The polyester army of Bible thumpers who harangue and solicit over the airwaves has led to further invocation of Mencken's ghost, as have the efforts of sanctimonious souls who call for the banning of books. Never sanguine about the future of his native land, Mencken suspected correctly that the American public would not grow more discriminating and that a menagerie of quacks would continue to compete garishly for money and publicity. Mencken never doubted that the task he performed so often would have to be undertaken by critics of future generations. Few, if any, have ever done it as well.

As a humorist, Mencken embraced all of America. The resident of Hollins Street who named his pet turtle "Mrs. Mary Baker Eddy" ranged easily, as a writer, from slapstick to black humor. Mencken was always more than willing to laugh at folly, especially when his fellow Americans became too serious, and hence far too confused, to laugh at themselves. If Mencken found little sacred, then it was for the simple reason, as he saw things, that little deserved to be. "One horse-laugh is worth ten thousand syllogisms," he explained. "It is not only more effective; it is also vastly more intelligent."[9] Fashions vary, Mencken well knew.

---

[9]Mencken, "The Iconoclast," in *Prejudices: Fourth Series* (New York: Knopf, 1924) 140.

Presidents come and go. Political parties rise and fall. What seems profound today may well seem preposterous tomorrow. The human animal, however, changes little. Mencken's laughter, like Mark Twain's, remains salubrious. To Mencken's credit, his iconoclasm extended to his own work. He despised special pleading and, unlike most people, genuinely felt more comfortable with censure than with praise. Mencken recognized that his mature writing, to say nothing of his early work, was widely uneven in quality. He knew that he wrote too much, but he saw from the beginning that his worst sin would have been silence about a matter that interested him. He never claimed that his thinking was profound. Some have found it commonplace; "commonsensical" would perhaps be a more accurate adjective. From our later vantage point, some of Mencken's polemical pieces can fail to convince. Mencken always viewed attack as the best defense; the fury of his assaults and his huge gifts as a stylist often hid, at least for the moment, a rhetorical technique that could be less than perfect. His political predictions were often laughable and some of his judgments about literature downright embarrassing. The man who railed at American provincialism was, on occasion, quite provincial himself. Mencken was neither devil nor demigod. Rather, he was a writer of immense talent who, much to his benefit, lived during an age that could appreciate his gifts. "I am often wrong," Mencken freely admitted to a correspondent in 1920. "My prejudices are innumerable, and often idiotic. My aim is not to determine facts—but to function freely and pleasantly—as Nietzsche used to say, to dance with arms and legs."[10] Few spectacles have so dazzled an American audience.

As a young poet, Mencken concluded that the fate of the man "who fought for the right" was oblivion, nothing more than a gravestone ravaged by time. His own career belied this lugubrious

---

[10]Mencken to Burton Rascoe, [Summer 1920?], in *Letters of H. L. Mencken*, ed. Guy J. Forgue (New York: Knopf, 1961) 187.

pronouncement. For half a century, no matter what role he was playing, Mencken's public life was characterized by bellicose individualism, unwavering pessimism, and considerable integrity. These qualities made him a national force in his day and memorable to posterity.

"I don't give a damn," Mencken once snorted to Theodore Dreiser, "what any American thinks of me."[11] This caustic statement was not idle rhetoric. Mencken told the truth as he saw it, without fear of the consequences. He cared not at all about being well liked, and this healthy indifference gained him considerable freedom, the liberty that allowed him to accomplish a great deal of good.

It is revealing that, as a young critic discussing Nietzsche, Mencken applauded the German's remarks about "fatalistic courage."[12] This courage born of despair marked Mencken's career. Willing to stand, alone if necessary, in the face of violent opposition, suspecting that any victories might well prove temporary, Mencken lambasted the proper opponents for half a century: ignorance, credulity, pretense, incompetence, dishonesty, and all types of censorship. He found the final two most odious. "The two main ideas," he explained, "that run through all my…writing are these: I am strongly in favor of liberty, and I hate fraud."[13]

He defended the right of authors to compose as they saw fit and the right of editors and publishers to seek writing of quality without regard to its moral tenor. In every available forum, he argued that political radicals, whose ideas he found preposterous, had the right to air their views. He battled for the right of

---

[11]Mencken to Theodore Dreiser, 8 November [1919], in *Dreiser-Mencken Letters: The Correspondence of Theodore Dreiser and H. L. Mencken, 1907–1945*, 2 volumes, ed. Thomas P. Riggio (Philadelphia: University of Pennsylvania Press) 360.
[12]Mencken, *The Philosophy of Friedrich Nietzsche* (Boston: Luce, 1908) 170.
[13]Mencken, "Autobiographical Notes, 1925," 165, EPFL.

individual citizens not to be harassed by those convinced that they know what is best for all and for the right of all Americans, regardless of race, to mingle freely in a public place. Mencken's defense of liberty was as non-partisan as it was unceasing. Many have claimed that their opponents deserve to be heard; Mencken actually meant it. It is this struggle against imposed silence and conformity, this vibrant celebration of the freedom to dissent, that marks Mencken's most enduring contribution to the land that gave him such a wealth of material and so much delight.

Afterword

H. L. Mencken was issued by the Continuum Publishing Company of New York City, during the spring of 1989, as part of its "Literature and Life: American Writers" series. Much has happened in the field of Mencken studies since that time. I am very pleased that, with this book being reissued by the Mercer University Press, I have the opportunity here to comment briefly upon some of these developments and to speculate about what the future might hold for the Sage of Baltimore.

For a variety of reasons, Mencken remains very much in the news. Part of this interest is due, of course, to the continuing appearance of new primary material. With the release, at various intervals, of a number of literary projects from time-lock, Mencken has managed his career quite skillfully from his grave. *My Life as Author and Editor*, edited by Jonathan Yardley, was published by Alfred A. Knopf in 1993. The next year, the Johns Hopkins University Press published *Thirty-Five Years of Newspaper Work: A Memoir by H. L. Mencken*. Both volumes contribute a substantial amount of information about these different aspects of Mencken's career. It was *The Diary of H. L. Mencken*, of course, that generated the most controversy and kept Mencken very much at the literary forefront. Edited by Charles A. Fecher, the *Diary* was published by Alfred A. Knopf in December 1989. On December 4 of that year, the Baltimore *Evening Sun* published Neil Grauer's "Mencken's 'Shocker,'" a lengthy front-page story that accused him of anti-Semitism.[1] This column was picked up by newspapers all across the land and generated a brouhaha on the American literary scene. The telephones in my

---

[1]Neil A. Grauer, "Mencken's 'Shocker,'" Baltimore *Evening Sun*, 4 December 1989.

home and in the Mencken Room at the Enoch Pratt Free Library seemed to ring incessantly until about March. Some of the indignant reporters actually seemed to have read the book. The letters-to-the-editor columns were filled with attacks and rebuttals; radio and television contributed further to the uproar. I wrote a lengthy essay-review for the *Virginia Quarterly Review*; I concluded then, and still believe now, that he was no anti-Semite.[2] Others have, of course, presented the opposing position very compellingly. Long in his grave, Mencken succeeded in generating huge controversy once more—controversy that has had, and will continue to have, an appreciable effect on Mencken scholarship. Any full-length study of the Baltimorean must now, I think, respond in some way to this issue of Mencken and anti-Semitism.

In addition to the appearance of material previously consigned to time-lock, other volumes have put primary material in public view. Mencken was an engaging and tireless correspondent—he wrote well over 100,000 letters—and four collections of these letters have appeared since the initial publication of this book: his correspondence with John Fante, edited by Michael Moreau and Joyce Fante; with Philip Goodman, edited by Jack Sanders; with Marion Bloom, edited by Edward A. Martin; and with the poet George Sterling, edited by S. T. Joshi. (In all, ten collections of letters have now been published.) Moreover, there have been a variety of collections of primary material published previously: such volumes as *The Impossible H. L. Mencken: A Selection of His Best Newspaper Stories*, edited by Marion Elizabeth Rodgers; *A Second Mencken Chrestomathy*, edited by Terry Teachout; *Mencken on Religion* and *Mencken on American Literature*, edited by S. T. Joshi and *H. L. Mencken: A Documentary Volume*, edited by Richard J. Schrader. With the appearance of such volumes, the American reading public has far

---

[2]Vincent Fitzpatrick, "After Such Knowledge, What Forgiveness?" *Virginia Quarterly Review* 66 (Summer 1990): 514–24.

easier access to Mencken's piquant commentary on a wide variety of topics. Moreover, a number of volumes have been translated for his readers abroad.[3] The secondary literature flourishes as well, for Mencken's life and work have been discussed frequently from a variety of perspectives in a variety of forums. Two substantial biographies (each very different from the other, both superb and eminently fair to Mencken) have appeared since 1989: Fred Hobson's *Mencken: A Life* (1994) and Terry Teachout's *The Skeptic: A Life of H. L. Mencken* (2002). A third biography, by Marion Elizabeth Rodgers, is forthcoming. Moreover, Mencken has been discussed in numerous books about other subjects. Clippings about the Baltimorean, primarily from newspapers but also from magazines and a variety of electronic sources, pour into the Mencken Room at an astonishing rate; they have filled over 1,000 large scrapbook pages in a calendar year. As part of its *American Writers* series, C-Span broadcast, live from Union Square in Baltimore City, a Mencken program that aired on 11 April 2002, was rebroadcast on the 15th, and is now available on the Internet.[4] It was a lively two hours. Callers responded from all across the land to comment on the merits and faults of one of the most controversial figures in American literary history. Wherever Mencken is now, he has to be delighted with all of the attention that he has been receiving.

---

[3]*Kulturkritische Schriften, 1918–1926*, vol. 1, [*Cultural Critical Works 1918–1926*], trans. by Helmut Winter (Leipzig: Manuscriptum, 1999); *Gesammelte Vorurteile* [*Collected Prejudices*], trans. with an afterword by Helmut Winter (Frankfurt am Main: Insel Verlag, 2000); *Autobiographisches 1930–1948*, vol. 2, [*Autobiographical Works* 1930–1948] trans. by Helmut Winter (Leipzig: Manuscriptum, 2000); and *Kommentare und Kolumnen 1909–1935* [*Commentaries and Columns 1908–1935*], ed. Helmut Winter, trans. by Joachim Kalka, Werner Schmitz, Heinrich Spies, Helmut Winter, and Hans Wolf (Leipzig: Manuscriptum 2002).

[4]"H. L. Mencken: *The American Language*." *American Writers II: The Twentieth Century*. Online. Internet. Website:http:www.americanwriters.org/writers/Mencken.asp.

Time runs on. We now find ourselves assessing Mencken's career more than 120 years after his birth. His final newspaper column appeared in the Baltimore *Sun* over fifty-five years ago. The Baltimore *Evening Sun*, the victim of changing circumstances, ceased publication on September 15, 1995. Mencken wrote his finest journalism for a newspaper that no longer exists. The Baltimorean's personal library, housed in Mencken Room, contains the books of a number of authors, once highly regarded, over whom the sands of time have washed. While it is enticing to say that art is long and life is short, it is not always true. Mencken's writing, on the other hand, remains very much alive, wondrously quotable and eminently topical. Ages hence, a new generation of readers will thrill to this remarkable prose that has outraged and delighted so many, will be dazzled as they watch this brazen Baltimorean "function freely and pleasantly" and "dance with arms and legs."[5] He will, I predict, continue to be reviled and revered. He is simply too immense to be ignored, far too vital to be forgotten.

---

[5] Mencken to Burton Rascoe, [Summer 1920?], in *Letters of H. L. Mencken*, ed. Guy J. Forgue (New York: Knopf, 1961) 187.

Bibliography

Because of limitations of space, the following bibliography is necessarily selective. In providing a very selective list of the magazines articles about Mencken, I have included earlier pieces as well as more recent ones, and both positive and negative assessments. Douglas C. Stenerson's *Critical Essays on H. L. Mencken* reprints a number of these articles and offers an informative discussion of the changing response to Mencken's canon. Those interested in a more comprehensive listing of the writing by and about Mencken should consult the following books. These bibliographies provide information about the various editions, reprints, and translations of Mencken's books and list unpublished masters' theses and doctoral dissertations about his writing. Many of the issues of *Menckeniana* carry a "Bibliographic Check List" that attempts to be as comprehensive as possible.

Adler, Betty, compiler, with the assistance of Jane Wilhelm. *H. L. M: The Mencken Bibliography*. Baltimore: Johns Hopkins University Press, 1961.

Adler, Betty, compiler. *H. L. M., The Mencken Bibliography: A Ten-Year Supplement, 1962–1971*. Baltimore: Enoch Pratt Free Library, 1971.

Bulsterbaum, Allison, compiler. *H. L. Mencken: A Research Guide*. New York: Garland Publishers, 1988.

Fitzpatrick, Vincent, compiler. *H. L. M.: The Mencken Bibliography: A Second Ten-Year Supplement, 1972–1981*. Baltimore: Enoch Pratt Free Library, 1986.

Schrader, Richard J., compiler, with the assistance of George H. Thompson and Jack R. Sanders. *H. L. Mencken: A Descriptive*

Bibliography. Pittsburgh Series in Bibliography. Pittsburgh: Pittsburgh University Press, 1998.

WORKS BY H. L. MENCKEN

Books and Pamphlets

Ventures into Verse. Baltimore: Marshall, Beck & Gordon, 1903.

George Bernard Shaw: His Plays. Boston: Luce, 1905.

The Philosophy of Friedrich Nietzsche. Boston: Luce, 1908.

The Artist: A Drama Without Words. Boston: Luce, 1912.

A Book of Burlesques. New York: Lane, 1916.

A Little Book in C Major. New York: Lane, 1916.

A Book of Prefaces. New York: Knopf, 1917.

Damn! A Book of Calumny. New York: Philip Goodman, 1918.

In Defense of Women. New York: Philip Goodman, 1918.

The American Language: A Preliminary Inquiry into the Development of English in the United States. New York: Knopf, 1919. Revised editions were published in 1921, 1923, and 1936. Supplements I and II were published in 1945 and 1948, respectively. An abridged version of the Fourth Edition and two Supplements, edited by Raven I. McDavid, Jr., was published by Knopf in 1963.

Prejudices: First Series. New York: Knopf, 1919.

Prejudices: Second Series. New York: Knopf, 1920.

Prejudices: Third Series. New York: Knopf, 1922.

Prejudices: Fourth Series. New York: Knopf, 1924.

Notes on Democracy. New York: Knopf, 1926.

Prejudices: Fifth Series. New York: Knopf, 1926.

Prejudices: Sixth Series. New York: Knopf, 1927.

Selected Prejudices. New York: Knopf, 1927.

Treatise on the Gods. New York: Knopf, 1930.

Making a President: A Footnote to the Saga of Democracy. New York: Knopf, 1932.

Treatise on Right and Wrong. New York: Knopf, 1934.

Erez Israel. New York: privately printed, 1935.

Happy Days: 1880–1892. New York: Knopf, 1940.

Newspaper Days: 1899–1906. New York: Knopf, 1941.

Heathen Days: 1890–1936. New York: Knopf, 1943.

Christmas Story. New York: Knopf, 1946.

The Days of H. L. Mencken: Happy Days, Newspaper Days, Heathen Days. New York: Knopf, 1947.

A Mencken Chrestomathy. New York: Knopf, 1949.

The Vintage Mencken. Edited by Alistair Cooke. New York: Vintage Books, 1955.

A Carnival of Buncombe. Edited by Malcolm Moose. Baltimore: Johns Hopkins University Press, 1956.

Minority Report: H. L. Mencken's Notebooks. New York: Knopf, 1956.

The Bathtub Hoax and Other Blasts & Bravos from the Chicago Tribune. Edited by Robert McHugh. New York: Knopf, 1958.

Prejudices: A Selection. Edited by James T. Farrell. New York: Vintage, 1958.

H. L. Mencken on Music: A Selection of His Writings on Music, Together with an Account of H. L. Mencken's Musical Life and a History of the Saturday Night Club. Edited by Louis Cheslock. New York: Knopf, 1961.

The American Scene: A Reader. Edited by Huntington Cairns. New York: Knopf, 1965.

H. L. Mencken's Smart Set Criticism. Edited by William H. Nolte. Ithaca, NY: Cornell University Press, 1968.

The Young Mencken: The Best of His Work. Edited by Carl Bode. New York: Dial Press, 1973.

A Gang of Pecksniffs: And Other Comments on Newspaper Publishers, Editors, and Writers. Edited by Theo Lippman, Jr. New Rochelle, NY: Arlington House, 1975.

Mencken's Last Campaign: H. L. Mencken on the 1948 Election. Edited by Joseph C. Goulden. Washington, DC: New Republic Book Company, 1976.

A Choice of Days. Edited by Edward L. Galligan. New York: Knopf, 1980.

The Editor, the Bluenose and the Prostitute: H. L. Mencken's History of the "Hatrack" Censorship Case. Edited by Carl Bode. Boulder, CO: Roberts Rinehart, 1988.

The Diary of H. L. Mencken. Edited by Charles A. Fecher. New York: Knopf, 1989.

The Gist of Mencken: Quotations From America's Critic. Edited by Mayo DuBasky. Metuchen, NJ: Scarecrow Press, 1990.

Tall Tales and Hoaxes of H. L. Mencken. Edited by John W. Baer. Annapolis, MD: Franklin Printing, 1990.

The Impossible H. L. Mencken: A Selection of His Best Newspaper Stories. Edited by Marion Elizabeth Rodgers. Garden City, NY: Doubleday, 1991.

My Life as Author and Editor. Edited by Jonathan Yardley. New York: Knopf, 1993.

Thirty-Five Years of Newspaper Work: A Memoir by H. L. Mencken. Edited by Fred Hobson, Vincent Fitzpatrick, and Bradford Jacobs. Baltimore: Johns Hopkins University Press, 1994.

A Second Mencken Chrestomathy. Edited by Terry Teachout. New York: Knopf, 1995.

H. L. Mencken on American Literature. Edited by S. T. Joshi. Athens, OH: Ohio University Press, 2002.

H. L. Mencken on Religion. Edited by S. T. Joshi. Amherst, NY: Prometheus Press, 2002.

Contributions to Books

Mencken, H. L. "Old Courthouses of Maryland." In *A Monograph of the New Baltimore Court House: One of The Greatest Examples of American Architecture, and the Foremost Court House of the United States, Including a Historical Sketch of the Early Courts of Maryland.* Baltimore: Frank D. Thomas, 1899.

Ibsen, Henrik. *A Doll's House.* Edited with an introduction and notes by H. L. Mencken. Boston: Luce, 1909.

Ibsen, Henrik. *Little Eyolf.* Edited with an introduction and notes by H. L. Mencken. Boston: Luce, 1909.

Nietzsche, Friedrich. *The Gist of Nietzsche.* Arranged by H. L. Mencken. Boston: Luce, 1910.

Men Versus the Man: A Correspondence Between Robert Rives La Monte, Socialist, and H. L. Mencken, Individualist. New York: Holt, 1910.

Hirshberg, Leonard Keene. *What You Ought to Know About Your Baby,* ghostwritten by Mencken. New York: The Butterick Company, 1910.

Mencken, H. L., George Jean Nathan, and Willard Huntington Wright. *Europe After 8:15.* New York: Lane, 1914.

Mencken, H. L. and George Jean Nathan. [Owen Hatteras, pseud.] *Pistols for Two.* New York: Knopf, 1917.

Mencken, H. L. and George Jean Nathan. *The American Credo: A Contribution Toward the Interpretation of the National Mind.* New York: Knopf, 1920.

Mencken, H. L. and George Jean Nathan. *Heliogabalus: A Buffoonery in Three Acts.* New York; Knopf, 1920.

Nietzsche, Friedrich Wilhelm. *The Antichrist.* Translated with an introduction by H. L. Mencken. New York: Knopf, 1920.

Mencken, H. L., editor. *Americana, 1925.* New York: Knopf, 1925.

Mencken, H. L., editor. *Americana,* 1926. New York: Knopf, 1926.

Mencken, H. L., editor. *Menckeniana: A Schimpflexikon.* New York: Knopf, 1928.

Huneker, James Gibbons. *Essays.* Selected with an introduction by H. L. Mencken. New York: Scribner, 1929.

Haardt, Sara Powell. *Southern Album.* Edited with a preface by H. L. Mencken. Garden City, NY: Doubleday, 1936.

Mencken, H. L. Preface to *Baltimore Yesterdays,* by Meredith Janvier. Baltimore: H. G. Roebuck & Son, 1937.

Mencken, H. L. Notes and introduction to *The Charlatanry of the Learned* by Johann Burkhardt Mencke. New York: Knopf, 1937.

Johnson, Gerald W., Frank R. Kent, H. L. Mencken, and Hamilton Owens. *The Sunpapers of Baltimore, 1837–1937.* New York: Knopf, 1937.

Mencken, H. L. Foreword to *By the Neck: A Book of Hangings,* edited by August Mencken. New York: Hastings House, 1942.

Mencken, H. L., editor. *A New Dictionary of Quotations on Historical Principles from Ancient and Modern Sources.* New York: Knopf, 1942.

Mencken, H. L. Introduction to *An American Tragedy,* by Theodore Dreiser. Cleveland and New York: World Publishing Company, 1946.

Mencken, H. L. "The American Language." In *Literary History of the United States,* edited by Robert E. Spiller, Willard Thorp, Thomas H. Johnson, and Henry Seidel Canby 663-675. New York: Macmillan, 1948.

Salzman, Jack, editor. *Theodore Dreiser: The Critical Reception.* New York: Lewis, 1972.

Bryer, Jackson R., editor. *F. Scott Fitzgerald: The Critical Reception.* New York: Burt and Franklin, 1978.

Mencken, H. L. *On Mencken.* Edited by John Dorsey. New York: Knopf, 1980.

Markel Howard, M.D and Frank A. Oski, M.D., editors. *The H. L. Mencken Baby Book: Comprising the Contents of H. L. Mencken's What You Ought To Know About Your Baby with Commentaries,* [ghostwritten by Mencken and published in 1910 under the byline of Leonard Keene Hirshberg]. Philadelphia: Hanley & Belfus, 1990.

Mencken, H. L. "Mencken and Nietzsche: An Unpublished Excerpt from Mencken's *My Life as Author and Editor.*" In *Dictionary of Literary Biography: Yearbook 1993,* excerpt edited by Terry Teachout 177-83. Detroit: The Gale Group/A Bruccoli Clark Layman Book, 1994.

Schrader, Richard J., editor. *H. L. Mencken, A Documentary Volume*. Volume 222 of *Dictionary of Literary Biography*. Detroit: The Gale Group/A Bruccoli Clark Layman Book, 2000.

Joshi, S. T., editor. *Atheism: A Reader*. New York: Prometheus Books, 2000. "On the Scopes Trial" 209-215.

Mencken, H. L. "Berlin, February, 1917." In *Dictionary of Literary Biography Yearbook, 2000*, article edited by Richard J. Schrader and Vincent Fitzpatrick. Detroit: The Gale Group/A Bruccoli Clark Layman Book, 2001. 195-213.

Correspondence

Letters of H. L. Mencken. Edited by Guy J. Forgue. New York: Knopf, 1961.

The New Mencken Letters. Edited by Carl Bode. New York: Dial Press, 1977.

Letters from Baltimore: The Mencken-Cleator Correspondence. Edited by P. E. Cleator. Rutherford, NJ: Fairleigh-Dickinson University Press, 1982.

Dreiser-Mencken Letters: The Correspondence of Theodore Dreiser & H. L. Mencken, 1907–1945, 2 volumes. Edited by Thomas P. Riggio. Philadelphia: University of Pennsylvania Press, 1986.

"Ich Kuss Die Hand": The Letters of H. L. Mencken to Gretchen Hood. Edited by Peter W. Dowell. University, AL: University of Alabama Press, 1986.

Mencken and Sara, A Life in Letters: The Private Correspondence of H. L. Mencken and Sara Haardt. Edited by Marion Elizabeth Rodgers. New York: McGraw-Hill, 1987.

John Fante & H. L. Mencken: A Personal Correspondence, 1930–1952. Edited by Michael Moreau and Joyce Fante. Santa Rosa, CA: Black Sparrow Press, 1989.

Do You Remember?: The Whimsical Letters of H. L. Mencken and Philip Goodman. Edited by Jack Sanders. Baltimore: Maryland Historical Society, 1996.

In Defense of Marion: The Love Letters of Marion Bloom and H. L. Mencken. Edited by Edward A. Martin. Athens, GA: University of Georgia Press, 1996.

From Baltimore to Bohemia: The Letters of H. L. Mencken and George Sterling. Edited by S. T. Joshi. Madison, NJ: Fairleigh Dickinson University Press, 2001.

SECONDARY SOURCES

Books About Mencken

Angoff, Charles. *H. L. Mencken: A Portrait from Memory.* New York: Yoseloff, 1966.

Bode, Carl. *Mencken.* Carbondale, IL: Southern Illinois University Press, 1969. Reprinted, with a new preface. Baltimore: Johns Hopkins University Press, 1986.

Boyd, Ernest. *H. L. Mencken.* New York: McBride, 1925.

Dorsey, John, editor. *On Mencken.* New York: Knopf, 1980.

Douglas, George H. *H. L. Mencken: Critic of American Life.* Hamden, CT: Archon Books, 1978.'

Fecher, Charles. *Mencken: A Study of His Thought.* New York: Knopf, 1978.

Forgue, Guy J. *H. L. Mencken: L'Homme, L'Oeuvre, L'Influence.* Paris: Minard, 1967.

Goldberg, Isaac. *The Man Mencken: A Biographical & Critical Survey.* New York: Simon And Schuster, 1925.

Harrison, S. L. *Mencken Revisited: Author, Editor & Newspaperman.* Lanham, MD: University Press of America, 1999.

Hatchett, Louis. *Mencken's Americana.* Macon, GA: Mercer University Press, 2001.

Hobson, Fred. *Mencken: A Life.* New York: Random House, 1994.

Hobson, Fred C., Jr. *Serpent In Eden: H. L. Mencken and the South.* Chapel Hill, NC: University of North Carolina Press, 1974.

Kemler, Edgar. *The Irreverent Mr. Mencken*. Boston: Little, Brown, 1950.

Manchester, William. *Disturber of the Peace: The Life of H. L. Mencken*. New York: Harper, 1950. Second edition, with a new introduction and envoi. Amherst, MA: University of Massachusetts Press, 1986.

Martin, Edward A. *H. L. Mencken and the Debunkers*. Athens, GA: University of Georgia Press, 1984.

Mayfield, Sara. *The Constant Circle: H. L. Mencken and His Friends*. New York: Delacorte, 1968.

Nolte, William. *H. L. Mencken: Literary Critic*. Middletown, CT: Wesleyan University Press, 1966.

Scruggs, Charles. *The Sage in Harlem: H. L. Mencken and the Black Writers of the 1920s*. Baltimore: Johns Hopkins University Press, 1984.

Singleton, M. K. *H. L. Mencken and the* American Mercury *Adventure*. Durham, NC: Duke University Press, 1962.

Stenerson, Douglas C. *H. L. Mencken: Iconoclast from Baltimore*. Chicago: University of Chicago Press, 1971.

Stenerson, Douglas C., editor. *Critical Essays on H. L. Mencken*. Boston: Hall, 1987.

Teachout, Terry. *The Skeptic: A Life of H. L. Mencken*. New York: HarperCollins, 2002.

Wagner, Philip. *H. L. Mencken*. Minneapolis: University of Minnesota Press, 1966.

Williams, W. H. A. *H. L. Mencken*. Boston: Twayne, 1977. Revised edition published as *H. L. Mencken Revisited*. Boston: Twayne, 1998.

Sections of Books About Mencken

Allen, Frederick Lewis. *Only Yesterday: An Informal History of the Nineteen-Twenties*. New York and London: Harper, 1931.

Brooks, Van Wyck. *The Confident Years: 1885–1915*. New York: Dutton, 1952.

Brugger, Robert J. *Maryland: A Middle Temperament, 1634–1980.* Baltimore: Johns Hopkins University Press, 1988.

Bulsterbaum, Allison. "Mencken, H. L." In *Encyclopedia of American Humorists*, volume 633 of *Garland Reference Library of the Humanities*, edited by Steven H. Gale 321-329. New York: Garland Publishing, 1988.

Cargill, Oscar. *Intellectual America: Ideas on the March.* New York: Macmillan, 1941.

Churchill, Allen. *The Literary Decade.* Englewood Cliffs, NJ: Prentice-Hall, 1971.

Conkin, Paul K. *When All the Gods Trembled: Darwinism, Scopes, and American Intellectuals.* Lanham, MD: Rowman & Littlefield, 1998.

Connolly, Thomas F. *George Jean Nathan and the Making of Modern America Drama Criticism.* Madison, NJ: Fairleigh Dickinson University Press, 2000.

Cooke, Alistair. *Six Men: Charles Chaplin, H. L. Mencken, Humphrey Bogart, Adlai Stevenson, Bertrand Russell, Edward VIII.* New York: Knopf, 1977.

Curtis, Thomas Quinn, *The Smart Set: George Jean Nathan & H. L. Mencken.* New York: Applause Books, 1997.

DeCasseres, Benjamin. *Mencken and Shaw: The Anatomy of America's Voltaire and England's Other John Bull.* New York: Silas Newton, 1930.

Dolmetsch, Carl R. *The Smart Set: A History and Anthology.* New York: Dial, 1966.

Douglas, George H. *The Smart Magazines: 50 Years of Literary Revelry at Vanity Fair, The New Yorker, Life, Esquire and The Smart Set.* Hamden, CT: Archon Books, 1991.

Dreiser, Theodore. *Letters of Theodore Dreiser: A Selection*, 2 volumes. Edited by Robert H. Elias. Philadelphia: University of Pennsylvania Press, 1959.

Egerton, John. *Speak Now Against the Day: The Generation before the Civil Rights Movement in the South.* New York: Knopf, 1994.

Epstein, Joseph. *Pertinent Players: Essays on the Literary Life.* New York: Norton, 1993.

Fecher, Charles A. "H. L. Mencken." In *Booknotes Life Stories: Notable Biographers on the People Who Shaped America,* edited by Brian Lamb 186-189. New York: Times Books, 1999.

Fitzpatrick, Vincent. "The *American Mercury.*" In *American Literary Magazine: The Twentieth Century,* edited by Edward E. Chielens 7-16. Westport: CT: Greenwood Press, 1992.

————. "The Bourgeois Baltimorean." In *Maryland: Unity in Diversity: Essays on Maryland Life and Culture,* edited by A. Franklin Parks and John B. Wiseman 182-195. Dubuque, IA: Kendall/Hunt, 1990.

————. *Gerald W. Johnson: From Southern Liberal to National Conscience.* Baton Rouge: Louisiana State University Press, 2002.

————. "H. L. Mencken (12 September 1880–29 January 1956)." In *Dictionary of Literary Biography,* volume 137 of *American Magazine Journalists, 1900–1960,* second series, edited by Sam G. Riley 179-204. Detroit: Gale Research/A Bruccoli Clark Layman Book, 1994.

————. "The Smart Set." In *American Literary Magazines: The Twentieth Century,* edited by Edward E. Chielens 333-341. Westport, CT: Greenwood Press, 1992.

Forman, Frank. *The Metaphysics of Liberty.* Dordrecht, Boston and London: Kluwer Academic Publishers, 1989.

Geismar, Maxwell. *The Last of the Provincials: The American Novel, 1915–1925.* Boston: Houghton, 1947.

Gold, Michael. *The Hollow Men.* New York: International Publishers, 1941.

Harrison, S. L. *Cavalcade of Journalists, 1900–2000.* Miami: Wolf Den Books, 2002.

————. *The Editorial Art of Edmund Duffy.* Madison and Teaneck, N.J.: Fairleigh Dickinson University Press, 1998.

Hays, Arthur Garfield. *Let Freedom Ring.* New York: Boni, 1928.

Henley, Ann. Introduction to *Southern Souvenirs: Selected Stories and Essays of Sara Haardt*. Tuscaloosa: University of Alabama Press, 1999.

Heuermann, Hartmut. "Henry Louis Mencken (1880–1956)." In *USA*, volume 2 of *Classics in Cultural Criticism*, edited by Hartmut Heuermann 195-226. Frankfort, New York, and Paris: Peter Lang, 1990.

Hicks, Granville. *The Great Tradition: An Interpretation of American Literature Since the Civil War*. New York: Macmillan, 1933.

Hitchens, Christopher. *Unacknowledged Legislation: Writers in the Public* Sphere. London: Verso, 2001.

Hobson, Fred. "H. L. Mencken (1880–1956)." In *Fifty Southern Writers After 1900: A Bio-Bibliographical Sourcebook*, edited by Joseph M. Flora and Robert Bain 313-323. Westport, CT: Greenwood Press, 1987.

———. Introduction to *South-Watching: Selected Essays by Gerald W. Johnson*. Chapel Hill: University of North Carolina Press, 1983.

———. "'This Hellawful South': Mencken and the Late Confederacy." In *Critical Essays on H. L. Mencken*, edited by Douglas C. Stenerson 174-185. Boston: Hall, 1987.

Hoffman, Frederick J. *The Twenties: American Writing in the Post-war Decade*. New York: Viking, 1955.

Hoopes, Roy. *Cain: The Biography of James M. Cain*. New York: Holt, Rinehart and Winston, 1982.

———. *Our Man in Washington*. New York: Forge, 2000.

Kazin, Alfred. *On Native Grounds*. New York: Reynal, 1942.

Larson, Edward J. *Summer for the Gods: The Scopes Trial and America's Continuing Debate Over Science and Religion*. New York: Basic Books, 1997.

Leary, Lewis. *Southern Excursions: Essays on Mark Twain and Others*. Baton Rouge: Louisiana State University Press, 1971.

Lehan, Richard. *Theodore Dreiser: The World of His Novels*. Carbondale, IL: Southern Illinois University Press, 1974.

Lewisohn, Ludwig. *Expressionism in America*. New York: Harper, 1932.

Lingeman, Richard. *Sinclair Lewis: Rebel from Main Street*. New York: Random House, 2002.

———. *Theodore Dreiser: An American Journey, 1908–1945*. Volume 2. New York: Putnam, 1990.

May, Henry F. *The End of Innocence: A Study of the First Years of Our Own Time, 1912–1917*. New York: Knopf, 1959.

Mott, Frank Luther. "The *American Mercury.*" In *A History of American Magazines*, volume 5 of *Sketches of 21 Magazines, 1905–1930*. 2-25 Cambridge, MA: Belknap Press of Harvard University Press, 1968.

———. *"The Smart Set."* In *A History of American Magazines*, volume 5 246-272. Cambridge, MA: Belknap Press of Harvard University Press, 1968.

Meyers, Jeffrey. *Edmund Wilson: A Biography*. Boston: Houghton Mifflin, 1995.

Nathan, George Jean. *The Intimate Notebooks of George Jean Nathan*. New York: Knopf, 1932.

———. "H. L. Mencken (1880–1956)." In *A George Jean Nathan Reader*, edited by A. L. Lazarus 173-180. Rutherford, NJ: Fairleigh Dickinson University Press, 1990.

Pattee, Fred Lewis. *Side-Lights on American Literature*. New York: Century, 1922.

Pritchard, William H. *Playing It By Ear: Literary Essays and Reviews*. Amherst, MA: University of Massachusetts Press, 1994.

Rascoe, Burton and Groff Conklin, editors. *The Smart Set Anthology*. New York: Reynal, 1934.

Rubin, Louis D. *The Mockingbird in the Gum Tree: A Literary Gallimaufry*. Baton Rouge: Louisiana State University Press, 1991.

Rubin, Louis D., editor. *The Comic Imagination in American Literature*. New Brunswick, NJ: Rutgers University Press, 1973.

Rubin, Louis D., Blyden Jackson, Rayburn S. Moore, Lewis P. Simpson, and Thomas Daniel Young, editors. *The History of Southern Literature.* Baton Rouge: Louisiana State University Press, 1985.

Ruland, Richard, *The Rediscovery of American Literature: Premises of Critical Taste, 1900–1940.* Cambridge, MA: Harvard University Press, 1967.

Schrader, Richard J., editor. *H. L. Mencken, A Documentary Volume.* Volume 222 of *Dictionary of Literary Biography.* Detroit: The Gale Group/A Bruccoli Clark Layman Book, 2000.

Scruggs, Charles. "H. L. Mencken and James Weldon Johnson: Two Men Who Helped Shape A Renaissance." In *Critical Essays on H. L. Mencken,* edited by Douglas C. Stenerson 186-203. Boston: Hall, 1987.

Sherman, Stuart Pratt. *Critical Woodcuts.* New York: Scribner, 1926.

Shivers, Frank. *Maryland Wits & Baltimore Bards: A Literary History with Notes on Washington Writers.* Baltimore: Maclay, 1985.

Swanberg, W. A. *Dreiser.* New York: Scribner, 1965.

Taylor, Kendall. *Sometimes Madness Is Wisdom: Zelda and Scott Fitzgerald, a Marriage.* New York: Ballantine Books, 2001.

Vidal, Gore. *United States: Essays, 1952–1956.* New York: Random House, 1993.

Williams, Harold A. *The Baltimore Sun: 1837–1987.* Baltimore: Johns Hopkins University Press, 1987.

Wilson, Edmund. *The Shores of Light: A Literary Chronicle of the Twenties and Thirties.* New York: Farrar, 1952.

Magazine Articles About Mencken

For all of the magazines except *Menckeniana,* the figure preceding the parentheses refers to volume number. For the Mencken quarterly, the figure refers to issue number.

Anderson, Fenwick. "Black Perspectives in Mencken's *Mercury.*" *Menckeniana* 70 (Summer 1979): 2–6.

Anderson, Mark. "H. L. Mencken and the Scopes Trial." *Tennessee Quarterly* 2 (Winter 1996): 50–64.

Atwell, Brother James, F. S. C. "Eclipse and Emergence," *Menckeniana* 24 (Winter 1967): 1–7.

Babbitt, Irving. "The Critic of American Life." *Forum* 79 (February 1928): 16–76.

Baker, Russell. "Me and Mencken." *Menckeniana* 127 (Fall 1993): 1–5.

Betz, Frederick. "'A German *Main Street*' and More: Heinrich Mann's *Der Untertan* (1918) and Sinclair Lewis's Satirical Novels of the 1920s." *MidAmerica* 27 (2000): 66–77.

———. "What's in a Name? Characterization and Caricature in Dorothy Thompson Criticism." (Syracuse University Library Associates) *Courier* 31 (1996): 51–74.

Bloom, Robert. "Past Indefinite: The Sherman-Mencken Debate on the American Tradition." *Western Humanities Review* 16 (Winter 1961): 73–81.

"Bouquets for Mencken." *The Nation* 177 (12 September 1953): 210–14.

Bourne, Randolph. "H. L. Mencken." *New Republic* 13 (24 November 1917): 102–03.

Butterfield, Roger. "Mr. Mencken Sounds Off." *Life* 21 (5 August 1946): 45–46, 48, 51–52.

Cain, William E. "A Lost Voice of Dissent: H. L. Mencken in Our Time." *Sewanee Review* 104 (Spring 1996): 229–47. Reprinted under the same title in *Menckeniana* 145 (Spring 1998): 1–11.

Cairns, Huntington. "The Quotable Mr. Mencken." *Menckeniana* 54 (Summer 1975): 8–10.

Chalberg, John C. "H. L. Mencken: Sage of Baltimore." *Maryland Humanities* [no volume number] (June 2002): 24–27.

Crowther, Hal. "MONEY, MEDIA, MYTHOLOGY: Mencken and the Maiming of America." *Meckeniana* 167 (Fall 2003): 1-13.

Dolmetsch, Carl. "'HLM' and 'GJN': The Editorial Partnership Re-examined." *Menckeniana* 75 (Fall 1980): 29–39.

———. "Mencken as Magazine Editor." *Menckeniana* 21 (Spring 1967): 1–8.

Dreiser, Theodore. "The Great American Novel." *American Spectator* 1 (December 1932): 1–2.

Duberman, Jason. "H. L. Mencken and the Wowsers." *American Book Collector* 7 (May 1986): 3–14.

Durr, Robert Allen. "The Last Days of H. L. Mencken." *Yale Review* 48 (Autumn 1958): 58–77.

Elliott, Leo. "Scopes Redux." *Menckeniana* 148 (Winter 1998): 1–8.

Emblidge, David. "H. L. Mencken's *In Defense of Women*." *Menckeniana* 61 (Spring 1977): 5–10.

Epstein, Joseph. "H. L. Mencken: The Art of Point of View." *Menckeniana* 71 (Fall 1979): 2–11.

———. "Our Favorite Cynic." *New Yorker* 72 (25 March 1996): 85–89.

Farrell, James T. "Notes Addressed to a Man Among the Angels." *Menckeniana* 18 (Summer 1966): 1–2.

Fecher, Charles A. "Firestorm: The Publication of H. L. Mencken's Diary." *Menckeniana* 113 (Spring 1990): 1–7.

———. "Mencken and the Sacred Sciences." *Menckeniana* 151 (Fall 1999): 7–14.

Fitzpatrick, Vincent. "After Such Knowledge, What Forgiveness?" *Virginia Quarterly Review* 66 (Summer 1990): 514–24.

———. "The Elusive Butterfly's Angry Pursuer: The Jamesian Style, Mencken, and Clear Writing." *Menckeniana* 59 (Fall 1976): 13–17.

———. "The Lady and the Tiger." *Virginia Quarterly Review* 64 (Spring 1988): 355–61.

————. "Wink Your Eye at Some Homely Girl: Misogyny and Mencken." *Menckeniana* 64 (Winter 1977): 4–10.

Forman, Frank. "Healthy Disrespect for Authority: The New Creationism." *Menckeniana* (Spring 2001): 1–7.

Fussell, Paul. "H. L. Mencken: Writer." *Menckeniana* 143 (Fall 1997): 1–7.

Goetz, Ruth Goodman. "The Faces of Enlightenment." *Menckeniana* 108 (Winter 1988): 1–6.

Grauer, Neil A. "Baltimore's Literary Heritage." *Maryland Humanities* [no volume number] (September 1998): 2–4.

Gutman, Arthur J. "The Mencken Society: A Chronicle." *Menckeniana* 140 (Winter 1996): 1–6.

Hamilton, Sharon. "The First *New Yorker*?: The *Smart Set* Magazine, 1900–1924." *Serials Librarian* 37 (1999): 89–104.

Harrison, S. L. "Anatomy of the Scopes Trial: Mencken's Media Event." *Menckeniana* 135 (Fall 1995): 1–6.

————. "Mencken and Duffy: Unique Artists." *Menckeniana* 153 (Spring 2000): 1–8.

————. "Mencken: Magnificent Anachronism." *American Journalism* 13 (Winter 1996): 60–78.

————. "Mencken Redoux." *Journal of American Culture* 13 (Winter 1990): 17–21.

Haubrich, William S. "Menckenisms." *Verbatim* 24 (Autumn 1999): 20–26. Reprinted under the same title in *Menckeniana* 158 (Summer 2001): 6–13.

Henley, Ann. "Sara Haardt and 'The Sweet, Flowering South.'" *Alabama Heritage* 31 (Winter 1994): 6–21. Reprinted under the same title, sans illustrations, in *Menckeniana* 129 (Spring 1994): 1–12.

Hitchens, Christopher. "Critic of the Booboisie." *Dissent* 41 (Summer 1994): 415–420.

Hobson, Fred. "Mencken's Blighted Violet: The Brief Career of Frances Newman." *Menckeniana* 60 (Winter 1976): 6–9.

————. "Mencken's 'Poet Born': John McClure of Oklahoma." *Menckeniana* 75 (Fall 1980): 40–43.

Holley, Val. "H. L. Mencken and the Indiana Genii." *Traces of Indiana and Midwestern History* 3 (Winter 1991): 4–15.

———. "The Sage and the Rabble-Rouser." *Maryland Humanities* [no volume number] (November/December 1994): 6–9.

Johnson, Gerald W. "H. L. Mencken (1880–1956)." *Saturday Review of Literature* 39 (11 February 1956): 12–13.

———. "Reconsideration: H. L. Mencken." *New Republic* 173 (27 December 1975): 32–33.

Joshi, S. T. "Letters: Mencken-Sterling." *Menckeniana* 155 (Fall 2000): 3–7.

———. "Mencken: Book Reviewer, 1908–1933." *Menckeniana* 160 (Winter 2001): 1–8.

Kazin, Alfred. "Mencken and the Great American Boob." *New York Review of Books* 34 (26 February 1987): 8–11.

Kempton, Murray. "Saving a Whale." *New York Review of Books* 28 (11 June 1981): 8, 10–12, 14.

Knopf, Alfred A. "H. L. Mencken, George Jean Nathan, and the *American Mercury*." *Menckeniana* 78 (Summer 1981): 1–10.

Kramer, Hilton. "H. L. Mencken, R.I.P." *National Review* 45 (12 April 1993): 54–56.

Krutch, Joseph Wood. "This Was Mencken: An Appreciation." *The Nation* 182 (11 February 1956): 109–10.

Lapham, Lewis H. "'If Only H. L. Mencken Were Still Alive.'" *Menckeniana* 139 (Fall 1996): 1–5. Published under the title "Painted Fire," *Harper's Magazine* 293 (November 1996): 11–15.

Lears, T. J. Jackson. "Ambivalent Victorian: H. L. Mencken." *Wilson Quarterly* 13 (Spring 1989): 112–18. Reprinted under the same title in *Menckeniana* 109 (Spring 1989): 1–7.

Lingeman, Richard. "Mencken, Dreiser and God." *Menckeniana* 119 (Fall 1991): 1–9.

Lippman, Walter. "H. L. Mencken." *Saturday Review of Literature* 3 (11 December 1926): 413–14.

McDavid, Raven I. "The Impact of Mencken on American Linguistics." *Menckeniana* 17 (Spring 1966): 1–7.

McDavid, Virginia. "Lines and Labels: Looking Back 50 Years." *Newsletter of the American Dialect Society* 28 (January 1996): 7–12.

McElroy, Wendy. "The Bathtub, Mencken, and War." *The Freeman* 49 (September 1999): 29–31.

Manchester, William. "The Last Years of H. L. Mencken." *Atlantic* 236 (October 1975): 82–90.

Markel, Howard, M.D. "What You Ought to Know About *What You Ought to Know About Your Baby*." *Menckeniana* 111 (Fall 1989): 7–13.

Martin, Edward A. "H. L. Mencken and Equal Rights for Women." *Georgia Review* 35 (Spring 1981): 65–76.

———. "The Ordeal of H. L. Mencken." *South Atlantic Quarterly* 61 (Summer 1962): 326–38.

Moseley, Merritt W. Jr. "H. L. Mencken and the First World War." *Menckeniana* 56 (Summer 1976): 8–15.

Motsch, Markus F. "H. L. Mencken and German Kultur." *German-American Studies* 6 (Fall 1973): 21–42.

Nardini, Robert F. "H. L. Mencken's *Ventures into Verse*." *South Atlantic Quarterly* 80 (Spring 1981): 195–205.

———. "Mencken and the 'Cult of Smartness.'" *Menckeniana* 84 (Winter 1982): 1–12.

Nolte, William H. "The Enduring Mencken." *Mississippi Quarterly* 32 (Fall 1979): 651–62.

Owens, Gwinn. "Mencken on Women." *Menckeniana* 64 (Winter 1977): 2–3.

Payne, Les. "Is Mencken Relevant to Blacks? Was He Ever?" *Menckeniana* 147 (Fall 1998): 1–9.

Pinsker, Sanford. "Stanley Crouch, Our Black American Mencken." *Virginia Quarterly Review* 74 (Summer 1998): 426–33.

Rampersad, Arnold. "Mencken, Race, and America." *Menckeniana* 115 (Fall 1990): 1–11.

Richman, Sheldon L. "The H. L. Mencken Diary: One Year Later." *Menckeniana* 117 (Spring 1991): 3–7.

———. "Mr. Mencken and the Jews." *American Scholar* 59 (Summer 1990): 407–411.

Riggio, Thomas P. "Dreiser and Mencken: In the Literary Trenches." *American Scholar* 54 (Spring 1985): 227–38.

Rodgers, Marion Elizabeth. "By His Own Rules." *Cigar Afficionado* [no volume number] (Summer 1994): 119-129.

———. "H. L. Mencken: The Young Professional." *Menckeniana* 111 (Fall 1989): 1–6.

———. "A Love Story: Mencken and Sara." *Maryland Humanities* [no volume number] (November/December 1994): 14–18.

Rubin, Louis D., Jr. "H. L. Mencken and the National Letters." *Sewanee Review* 74 (Summer 1966): 723–38.

———. "An Honorable Profession: H. L. Mencken and the News." *Menckeniana* 131 (Fall 1994): 1–11.

Sanders, Jack R. "Mencken and Goodman." *Menckeniana* 137 (Spring 1996): 1–8.

———. "Stormy Days." *Maryland Humanities* [no volume number] (November/December 1994: 3–5.

Schaum, Melita. "H. L. Mencken and American Cultural Masculinism." *Journal of American Studies* 29 (December 1995): 379–98. Reprinted under the same title in *Menckeniana* 142 (Summer 1997): 1–14.

Schrader, Richard J. "But 'Gentlemen Marry Brunettes': Anita Loos and H. L. Mencken." *Menckeniana* 98 (Summer 1986): 1–7.

———. "Mencken and Other Lone Eagles." *Menckeniana* 156 (Winter 2000): 1–11.

Schwartz, Gerald. "The West as Gauged by H. L. Mencken's *American Mercury*." *Menckeniana* 89 (Spring 1984): 1–14.

Sedgwick, Ellery III. "HLM, Ellery Sedgwick, and the First World War." *Menckeniana* 68 (Winter 1978): 1–4.

Sherman, Stuart Pratt. "Beautifying American Literature." *The Nation* 105 (29 November 1917): 593–94.

Shivel, Gail. "Sara Haardt: Her Neglected Writings of the South." *Menckeniana* 128 (Winter 1993): 4–7.

Shutt, James W. "H. L. Mencken and the Baltimore *Evening Sun* Free Lance Column," *Menckeniana* 48 (Winter 1973): 8–10.

Stenerson, Douglas C. "Baltimore: Source and Sustainer of Mencken's Values." *Menckeniana* 41 (Spring 1972): 1–9.

————. "The 'Forgotten Man' of H. L. Mencken." *American Quarterly* 18 (Winter 1966): 686–96.

————. "Mencken's Early Newspaper Work: The Genesis of a Style." *American Literature* 37 (May 1965): 153–66.

————. "Mencken's Efforts to Reshape Dreiser as Artist and Man." *Dreiser Studies* 21 (Spring 1990): 2–20.

————. "Short-Story Writing: A Neglected Phase of Mencken's Literary Apprenticeship." *Menckeniana* 30 (Summer 1969): 8–13.

Stevens, Ray. "Rattling the Subconscious: Joseph Conrad and the Mencken Controversy." *Menckeniana* 132 (Winter 1994): 1–12.

Teachout, Terry. "What Would They Think of the 90s?" *American Enterprise* 10 (November–December 1999): 18–19.

Van Doren, Carl. "Smartness and Light: H. L. Mencken, a Gadfly for Democracy." *The Century* 105 (March 1923): 791–96.

Vass, Mary Miller and James L. W. West III, "The Composition and Revision of Mencken's *Treatise on the Gods.*" *Papers of the Bibliographical Society of America* 77 (Fourth Quarter 1983): 447–61. Reprinted under the same title in *Menckeniana* 88 (Winter 1983): 9–16.

Vidal, Gore. "The Essential Mencken." *The Nation* 253 (26 August–2 September 1991): 228-33.

Weeks, Edmund. "The *Atlantic* Bookshelf." *Atlantic Monthly* 165 (March 1940):n. p.

Weigel, George. "God, Man, and H.L. Mencken," *First Things* 53 (May 1995): 50-59. Reprinted under the same title in *Menckeniana* 134 (Summer 1995): 1-12.

Welshko, Thomas G. "The Free Lance (I)" and "The Free Lance (II)". *Menckeniana* 69 (Spring 1979): 1–12; and 70 (Summer 1979): 11–14.

Wilson, Edmund. "H. L. Mencken." *New Republic* 27 (1 June 1921): 10–13.

Woodward, C. Vann. "Baltimore's Mencken." *Menckeniana* 136 (Winter 1995): 1–6.

Wycherley, H. Alan. "'Americana': The Mencken-Lorimer Feud." *Costerus* 5 (1972): 227–36.

Permissions

The author and publisher are grateful for permission to draw upon the author's writing that appeared previously in:

H.L.M., The Mencken Bibliography: A Second Ten-Year Supplement, 1972–1981. Baltimore: Enoch Pratt Free Library, 1986

Menckeniana

Virginia Quarterly Review.

Writing by Theodore Dreiser is quoted with the kind permission of the Dreiser Trust and the University of Pennsylvania.

Writing by H.L. Mencken is quoted with the kind permission of the Enoch Pratt Free Library in accordance with the terms of the will of Henry Louis Mencken.

Index

Works are by H. L. Mencken unless otherwise noted. HLM in the index refer to Henry Louis Mencken.